What America Needs to Survive

to Survive

Thoughts, Ideas, and Solutions

Jeff Bradford

ISBN-13: 978-0615612201

Publisher: Amazon.com Inc. / JCB Publishing

TABLE OF CONTENTS

INTRODUCTION

Howdy friend! Yes you. If you are an American, I consider you my friend until such time as you give me a reason to feel otherwise. And even then, I'll respect your right to feel and be any way you like—so long as your actions don't infringe on the rights of others. Why do I feel this way? Because I believe in our Founding Fathers' beliefs in unalienable rights and that you are an invaluable part of this country I love. The unalienable rights of the people are why this country was founded and created. My name is Jeff Bradford, and I have been driven to write this book because of my growing concern over this country that I love. This concern has developed over the last few years as I have been interested in educating myself about the early revolutionary history of our country. As I have been enlightened by my new understanding of our country and the righteous, sometimes eternal principles it was founded upon, I have realized that our government has shifted from some of these principles. In many respects we no longer have a government whose primary concern is to *support the people* but we have slowly returned to that form of government whose primary concern is *how the people can support the government*. That type of thinking and focus in government is why our Founding Fathers stood up and fought the American Revolution in the first place! I'm sure there are a few of you out there who are chuckling right now and are thinking, "Welcome aboard!" Well, I don't blame you for feeling that way, but all I can say is, "Here I am now!" Better late than never, I guess. My new understanding and appreciation for the principles that our country was founded upon, as well as appreciation for our Founding Fathers, generations of veterans, and patriotic American families, have left me with a desire to honor them by doing my part to support, defend, and reestablish (if necessary) the principles that they stand and stood for. I admire all that they did and do and I aspire to be like them as much as I can. I can no longer idly sit by and hope for the best for our country. That is not what I believe our Founders Fathers would do and for me to even be a little bit like them I must commit myself and my beliefs into action as they did. The writing of this book is a step in that commitment to express my love for this country through my actions.

Initially, it was my intent to review enough history about the Founding Fathers, our country, and the constitution they created that there would be a fairly clear picture of the beginnings of our country to establish a reference of where we came from. In the interest of time, I have decided to condense and paraphrase as much information as possible so as to expedite this effort. In so doing, I understand that this book won't give our history the justice it deserves, but I feel it is imperative that I get these political thoughts and ideas before the American public prior to this coming 2012 presidential election. I apologize for the method by which I am referencing supporting works as a credible source for my beliefs; I will list my sources, but the reader might be left to research those sources cited. My desire to get these thoughts and ideas before the American people outweigh my desire to make this endeavor flawless before literary peers.

My concern has left me feeling that another four years of inaction could be devastating to our country. As a nation, we are at the point that we can't even make it through one fiscal budget year without raising our debt ceiling to another all-time high. Do we think that our government will be cheaper to operate next year? With the track record of our government lately, do we believe that a sudden moral change of character and fiscal responsibility will come over us and protect us from having to raise our debt ceiling again next year and every year after that? How far will our debtors allow us to go before they are rightfully entitled to repossess their debt and what does that mean for our country? Can we file bankruptcy on the world and expect there won't be some form of retaliation or consequence? Do we currently see or hear any real initiatives to stop and prevent the corruption of "pork barrel" and backroom politics? I have talked with many friends and citizens about what they think can be done for what ails our country and, after they have vented their frustrations, they almost always end up with the assessment that there's nothing that can be done. "The problems are too big and the government is too corrupt," they say. The fact that a majority of us feel this way is a huge indicator that, "Houston, we have a problem!" We have or have had most of the fundamental rights, checks and balances to sustain our country indefinitely, but we are in dire need of some surgical adjustments or the cancer that is currently afflicting us will eventually take over the whole country, not just the government. Our government is off course and needs a course correction quick before it gets so far off track that the gravitational pull of the patriotic people in this country won't be enough to get us back on course! We don't want to end up in that black hole called "indentured servitude" to our government or the governments of the world that we owe our debt to!

The average lifespan of democratic governments in history has been approximately 300 years. Likewise, we run the risk of being another statistic in history if we don't seriously examine our flaws and correct them for the good of our country--not for our political party, ethnicity, religion, or special interests. As we head into our third century of existence, we had better evaluate our shortcomings and the potential they have to damage or cause our society to fail. If we continue on in the downward trend we are taking, eventually we will collapse and fail. The fact that we started on good ground only means that it might take a little longer to crash, and without proper course corrections along the way, we will eventually fail as other societies in history have done. Denial will lead us right into failure's mouth until it closes down around us and we have no escape from the inevitable.

We need to reanalyze, as a society, why civilizations in the past have failed, so as to not repeat history. As prolific researchers of history, our Founding Fathers knew these things and made provisions for us to correct our course, when needed, so as to not suffer the fate of the failed governments and societies in history. Our Founding Fathers researched and chose wisely. What things have changed in our government since its founding? Have these changes put our government at risk of failure through imbalances of power and corruption? Have changes in society produced issues that need to be addressed in our government—issues our Founding Fathers could not have foreseen or made provision for in our constitution? Do the amendments we've made to our constitution support sound reasoning for the good of the whole, or have they crept in slowly through "pork barrel" politics to benefit the few at the expense of the whole? All of the amendments to our Constitution, from its beginning until now, need to be reevaluated to see if they stand up to standards that are good for the whole and not just the few. That's not to say that minorities should be overlooked. Our Founding Fathers were very concerned over the plight of the minority and made provision for such, but a standard that supports the betterment of all in society, to include minorities, should be adopted for the good of the whole not just a select few. As we have dealt with these new societal issues, have we patterned our method of finding sound solutions on the diligent research and debate that our Founding Fathers used to produce sound solutions as they did? Is our government putting aside party politics and legislating for the good of the whole as our Founding Fathers did?

Ancient Israel, Rome, and the Anglo-Saxon nations all survived for several hundred years as effective republics. Thomas Jefferson once said about the Anglo-Saxon nation, its form of government and its laws, that it was ". . . *the wisest and most perfect ever yet devised by the wit of man.*"[1] Jefferson, Madison, and others incorporated many of these qualities into our constitution and government. Why did they incorporate these governmental qualities? It was because that throughout the history of man these are the ones that succeeded and survived the longest. They had the best record. They read history and learned from it! One of the reasons they compromised and worked so hard to create a united government was they realized that as a united nation, we had a chance of standing strong and surviving. But if we were divided, we would be forever weakened and eventually fail. They also saw an opportunity to create and reestablish a proper form of government that represented the people in a way that the world hadn't seen in over a thousand years. So that freedom might spill over from our borders to benefit the world, they diligently worked to hammer out every detail to the best of man's ability. They acknowledged a few flaws in their work, but secured every good principle that could be had to the benefit of our country within the scope of what society could bear at the time. They pushed the envelope on issues that were ingrained into the society of their time. Slavery was a hot topic that tried the moral conscience of many during the Constitutional Convention and was compromised on in an effort to secure the best government they could get at the time for our country. Eventually, this festering moral cancer had to be overcome to put our country back into alignment with the Providential Power that helped establish this great country. There are a few other issues that were not dealt with at the time, either, because those issues didn't exist then and couldn't be foreseen—or they were constrained by the circumstances of what society could bear at the time.

We were fledgling states then that were still in our infancy; we weren't sure what we wanted at the time. Not all but some states struggled with supporting a national government during our American Revolution, hence, some of the deplorable conditions the Continental Army had to endure to survive. As we were throwing off the yoke of

Mother England, we were reluctant to support another parental yoke such as was proposed in the federal government. As states, we were somewhat juvenile in wanting things our way, with barely having polite regard for the fate of others. Our constitution and form of government gave us the parental guidance, direction, and protection we needed to grow and evolve into the mature United States that we are today. No longer is there the hesitation to support our government as a whole and now we are even found to be proud and honored to do so. We've been through so much together in the last two hundred plus years that the thought of not being a United States is almost nonexistent. We had better not take for granted the blessing that being a *United States* has been to our country and we had better not be deceived to believe that we can reclaim those blessings once they are lost. We MUST preserve what we have been blessed with. Our liberties, our posterity, and our country are counting on us to do it.

I dedicate this book to my Lord and Savior Jesus Christ, our Founding Fathers, patriotic American families and citizens, my family, and anyone else worldwide who has supported freedom anywhere in the world. You all have made it possible for someone like me to write and publish something like this. You have my love and appreciation.

CHAPTER ONE

SOME HISTROY, BELIEFS, AND CONCERNS

Thomas Jefferson was a prolific researcher and scholar. He not only had an insatiable desire to know and understand his world but he dug deep to know and understand where his world came from and how it had gotten there. Jefferson's thorough study of the governments and societies, which have existed in the history of the world, gave him a deep understanding and a knowledgeable reference as to the structure required to create a government capable of having the best chance of happiness and success. Although he wasn't a delegate to the Constitutional Convention of 1787, his thoughtful writing of the Declaration of Independence and his many communications to Convention delegates greatly influenced the content of what was written into our constitution.

James Madison, known as the "Father of the Constitution," was an exceptional scholar, historian, and politician as well—one that was capable of thoroughly digesting an idea from his colleagues then determining the value of that idea and the effect it might on the government they were trying to create. He had a knack for converting theoretical ideas, values, and principles into practical applications within governmental structure, while maintaining his focus on the lessons he had gleaned from his research of governments and societies in history. He had vision and focus backed up by tireless research and vast knowledge. He not only understood the things he learned, but knew how to apply them, implement and give them value.

George Washington has been called the "Father of our Country" and rightfully so. Washington committed and sacrificed all that he could to support and defend his countrymen. Not only did he commit many of his worldly possessions, but he thoroughly committed himself through his involvement and actions as a politician, a military man, and an ordinary citizen. Courage, integrity, honesty, gratitude, commitment, and action were qualities that he shared to the benefit of all those around him. His influences as a politician, military man, and citizen were found to be very thoughtful and when he found it necessary to commit to a course of action, Washington was commonly found to be taking the lead in the actions that needed to be taken. He either brokered or led numerous military and political initiatives in support of the ideals he believed in to the betterment of his country.

Most, if not all, of the Constitutional delegates were accomplished scholars with deep educational and religious backgrounds that came from applying themselves to traditional and/or personal education and research. Most, if not all of them, acknowledged and recognized the providential help from God in support of the freedoms, country, and government they were founding. Most were considered the best men available to represent their state and secure the interest of their states and the country.

There were countless other heroic men, women, and children throughout this country who committed themselves through the sacrifices of their time, their talents, their means, their possessions, and, in many instances, their lives in support of their families, their neighbors, their countrymen, and their country without regard for benefit of any kind. Their benefit was the joy of serving others they loved and the peace that comes from having done the right thing within their hearts and minds.

After exhausting, thorough debate and compromise, our constitution was written with the purpose of securing every good right and principle that could be obtained within the bounds of what society could accept at the time. It was also written with the understanding that if they didn't address and protect our government from the weaknesses of mankind, that their newfound government would not hold up and survive; it would repeat the failures of governments and societies in history if certain rights were not secured and the government were not properly structured and restrained. It was this spirit of securing the rights they felt they *hud* to have, while being flexible on issues they *wanted* to have, and protecting those rights from the corrupt tendencies of man that gave them an effective formula for producing a Constitution and legislation whose overall focus was securing those rights for the good of the whole while protecting the necessary rights of the few.

Our Constitution was set up with checks and balances to prevent corruption and the consolidation of power in our government from *People's Law*, toward *Ruler's Law (tyranny)*, or toward *No Law (anarchy)*. [2] The power of our government was intended and structured originally to be with the *people first*, the *states second*, and the *federal government third*--in that order. Is there anybody left in America today that feels like the hierarchy or order of power and control in our country is *the people are in control* followed by *the states are in control* and then by *the federal government is in control*? If the answer in your gut says no, then you feel there has been a major shift in governmental power from *People's Law* toward *Ruler's Law* since our country began. Let's assess this monumental issue for a minute. Are we more accountable to the federal government than the federal government is accountable to us? Are we more accountable to our states than they are accountable to us? We have the power to vote, but do they provide us with the transparency of information to be informed voters or are they operating under the cover of dense bureaucracy that leaves the voter to hope that the media will provide the information required to be an informed voter? Who benefits from the people being uninformed or under informed as voters? The government benefits by being allowed to shift the balance of power in their direction while we sit by in an uninformed stupor. Who benefits from voters being informed? The people benefit by keeping in place those checks and balance that keep the power in our government with the people.

Some people I have talked with about this subject believe that, as responsible citizens, people should research, know, and understand our political issues and the candidates or representatives that operate our government. While I agree with this premise, statistics show it is not realistic. As a country, our average quadrennial voting participation percentages from 1960 to 2008 were approximately 55 percent. I believe that of those people who did participate, the percentage of people who do the research required to be informed voters are a minority. Because of this vacuum of under-informed voters we are left with the majority of us voting on candidates based on their looks, what we hear them say, possibly a debate or two, what we might hear on TV or radio, their name, advertisements, and our feelings about that person. As a society we are leaving the operation of our country to chance in the hopes that those we've elected will perform their duties honorably and in our best interest. I have a political secret to share with you: in a lot of instances, it's not working! We have repeated examples of party politics and corruption that has personal and special interests at heart and not the good of the country. Many of our politicians are more focused on themselves, the good of their political party, the good of those in influence who can help their initiatives, and lastly the good of the country if it fits into their higher priorities.

In the interest of preserving our freedoms, retaining power in our government with the people and giving us the best chance of making informed decisions about our president, Supreme Court justices, congressional representatives, and ballot initiatives, I believe that we should receive an annual accounting, in synopsis and lay format, of all the votes, decisions, bills, and executive orders handed down by our government. To protect our freedoms, our country, and for sustainment of our future, our government needs to be accountable to the people and their vote. As uninformed voters the balance of power will continue to shift towards the government, corruption will eventually and completely overrun us, and eventually we will lose the freedoms and opportunities that we have been blessed with.

At this point, I feel it is appropriate to interject some feelings and beliefs from a couple of our Founding Fathers. John Adams said:

"There is nothing which I dread so much as a division of the republic into two great parties, each arranged under its leader, and concerting measures in opposition to each other. This, in my humble apprehension, is to be dreaded as the greatest political evil under our constitution."

Wow, how insightful and inspired was that statement? Is there anybody left in America that wouldn't agree our government has shifted from having a common goal and purpose for the people and has moved toward special interests for themselves, their political party, and the government? It didn't take long for the interest of the country to be replaced by party politics and political agendas. As a country we are great at pulling together in the face of adversity or a declared, common enemy, such as in a war or crisis, but we struggle to come together in the name of prosperity and happiness. Well, our prosperity and freedoms are at risk--they are losing ground fast and we are gaining an increasingly burdensome government. If we don't rally together soon it could be too late. The damage done could be too great to overcome.

Listen closely to this next inspired statement. After having seen the effects of two party politics upon our country, George Washington said this in his farewell speech to the nation:

"The alternate domination of one faction over another, sharpened by the spirit of revenge, natural to party dissension, which in different ages and countries has perpetrated the most horrid enormities, is itself a frightful despotism. But this leads at length to a more formal and permanent despotism. The disorders and miseries, which result, gradually incline the minds of men to seek security and repose in the absolute power of an individual; and sooner or later the chief of some prevailing faction, more able or more fortunate than his competitors, turns this disposition to the purposes of his own elevation, on the ruins of Public Liberty.

Without looking forward to an extremity of this kind, (which nevertheless ought not to be entirely out of sight,) the common and continual mischief's of the spirit of party are sufficient to make it the interest and duty of a wise people to discourage and restrain it.

It serves always to distract the Public Councils, and enfeeble the Public Administration. It agitates the Community with ill-founded jealousies and false alarms; kindles the animosity of one part against another, foments occasionally riot and insurrection. It opens the door to foreign influence and corruption, which find a facilitated access to the government itself through the channels of party passions. Thus the policy and the will of one country are subjected to the policy and will of another.

There is an opinion, that parties in free countries are useful checks upon the administration of the

Government, and serve to keep alive the spirit of Liberty. This within certain limits is probably true; and in Governments of a Monarchical cast, Patriotism may look with indulgence, if not with favor, upon the spirit of party. But in those of the popular character, in Governments purely elective, it is a spirit not to be encouraged. From their natural tendency, it is certain there will always be enough of that spirit for every salutary purpose. And, there being constant danger of excess, the effort ought to be, by force of public opinion, to mitigate and assuage it. A fire not to be quenched, it demands a uniform vigilance to prevent its bursting into a flame, lest, instead of warming, it should consume."

There was concern--if not fear-- by some of the Founding Fathers that two party politics would cause self-interest and corruption. When you have only two parties, there is no need of compromise but only to win the contest between the two parties. When there are more than two parties involved, then the situation requires allegiances and compromise if one has any hope of being successful. That's why the Constitutional Convention was so successful in creating such profound legislation because there were 13 different parties which required allegiance and compromise for the good of the whole. The other 12 parties wouldn't have stood by or accepted legislation that was good for just one party's self-interested initiatives. Consider this; if we choose and trust a 12 person jury of our peers to judge the adherence of our laws then why wouldn't we extend that standard upstream to require organized diversity of thought and representation in the creation of our laws by our legislators? Two political parties are not diverse enough to foster compromise. Diversity of thought and representation beyond two parties creates the need to truly listen, understand and compromise which can create results beneficial to all. That recipe of organizational structure and diversity of opinion created our constitution. Although our Founding Fathers had many differences of opinion, they had the spirit of patriotism and compromise to put the interest of the country before their own agendas. Then we had thirteen parties (states), there wasn't a dominance of party power and politics that invites self-interest and corruption. There wasn't a political stalemate of one party against the other with their own party agendas the primary focus of government instead of the good of the country. The obtainment and control of power can be a very corruptive influence and needs to be dispersed. Otherwise, one's focus can be distracted from the issues at hand and possibly diverted to the obtainment of power to force their agendas on the people. Forcing party solutions on our country is a limited form of controlled tyranny. It's when we compromise for the good of all concerned that we represent the majority while protecting the minority.

Thomas Jefferson said:

"When all government, domestic and foreign, in little as in great things, shall be drawn to Washington as the center of all power, it will render powerless the checks provided of one government on another and will become as venal and oppressive as the government from which we separated."

Is there anyone out there in our country who doubts that the center of power in our country has been drawn to Washington? I believe there is an effective way of interjecting a *people's vote of conscience* to break up the corruptive and self- indulgent effects of the concentration of power in Washington and the political parties we have today, which I will describe in more detail in Chapter 3.

I believe there are still some good, honorable, politicians out there that are trying to do the right thing. But what's wrong with reinstating or giving them some boundaries to operate by? Boundaries that give them the freedom to legislate in our best interest but would be designed to protect us if they don't. It's clear that our Founding Fathers had every expectation that our country and Constitution would grow and evolve. They didn't have the opportunity or life span to address all the issues that would come up--and in many instances, we've made some legislative mistakes on our own. The process and mentality of focusing on the good of the whole, while considering and protecting the few, is a useful tool for evaluating current and past legislation. "Pork barrel" politics is coercive, corrupt, and needs to be stopped before its excesses and waste runs our country into the ground. We need to evaluate and use those processes that our Founding Fathers used to filter our legislation for the betterment of our country.

The circumstances of our country will change over time. Change is inevitable; the process of evaluating what changes need to be made can be refined to principles and processes that apply over time with only minor future adjustments. We just need to ask the right questions to reveal the intent, purpose, benefit, or consequence behind proposed legislation. Those types of processes need to be amended into our constitution so that we're not so reliant upon the integrity of our politicians. Let's face it--some of them haven't been so honorable and full of integrity. There are some modern, valuable, process improvement models, root cause analysis methods, and improved ways of determining the value of what is being considered by our government--ways that the private sector have been benefiting from for decades. Granted, looking into our constitution, government, and the way it operates is a delicate thing that should be done carefully and with all solemnity. But our country is at a juncture where if we don't try to correct the error of our ways, we run the risk of collapse. We need thoughtful and inspired action now before its too late. Considering our current state of the union, I believe our Founding Fathers wouldn't have hesitated to act, and I feel that we should act as well. We should act in profound ways that are not just lip service to the political mantra for change but in ways that change our course and heal our country for a sustained future for our posterity and the country we love.

CHAPTER TWO

PERSONAL GOVERNMENT EXPERIENCES

This chapter covers some of the many different experiences I've had with our government and some of the conclusions those experiences have left me with. Let me first start by saying that not all, but most, politicians come from wealth and means. Many of their views and opinions are formulated by having received secondhand information from somewhere other than personal experiences of what's happening at the grass roots level in our country. Opinions of others, statistics, news media reports, and external information they have received from others color their positions on how best to deal with the problems our country faces. Because they haven't lived with these problems, and unless they're willing to do the necessary research and homework that our Founding Fathers did, this can be a serious handicap for them and their ability to create real solutions. Without experience, they don't have sufficient knowledge of what our problems really are to formulate effective solutions. To them it's all hypothetical scenarios they have never really experienced. Sympathy can only take you so far down the road of true understanding and knowledge. Sorry, guys, for the following example: but as much as we try to relate to what it must feel like to be pregnant, we will never truly understand what that feels like or means physically, emotionally, mentally, and spiritually. Likewise, as a politician, if you have never lived in the bowels of this country and have lived first-hand some of the successes and failures of this country, your understanding of what's required to heal this country will lean heavily on the hypothetical and away from realistic, workable solutions.

One of my earlier federal government experiences was while I was working as a helicopter mechanic for a company that was contracted by the Bureau of Land Management (BLM). The job was to count goats that live near Deming, New Mexico. These goats, as I remember, were supposed to be the bloodline or DNA ancestors of the original goats from Iran. The helicopter pilot and a spotter on board were supposed to count the goats. The BLM district in that area was appropriated, by Congress, 50 hours of flying time that fiscal year to count these goats. We finished the job within ten hours--and that was taking our time a little bit. Then the BLM proceeded to have us fly every secretary, relative, and friend sightseeing for the remaining 40 hours so that the BLM outpost would get the same appropriation of helicopter flight time the next fiscal year. Approximately $40,000.00 was wasted on government sightseeing, at a very small BLM outpost, with a handful of employees. It was then I wondered and realized that if this little BLM outpost can waste that much money, how many other entities of government agencies are out there, in our country, who are all trying to spend their appropriated allotment so that they can get at least the same amount of money next year? I'll bet the real amount is staggering. I have given our appropriations system some considerable thought and my conclusion in the end is no matter what system of funds disbursement our government chooses, if federal employees are allowed to waste government money without fear of real consequences, then these abuses will continue to happen no matter what system we operate under. We need real consequences of law, which are enforced at every level, to deter the misappropriation of taxpayer funds by every organization in government.

Another federal government experience I've had is with the U.S. Forest Service (USFS). These experiences are more environmental policy-related than they are financial, but the effects still revolve around government waste. As a helicopter mechanic I have been involved in many helicopter logging operations that have involved the USFS. Most commercial operators of civilian managed, forested lands will only take and cut their trees down to a minimum merchantable size or diameter that can be processed at the receiving timber mill. To take anything smaller would waste a tree that has the potential of producing wood products in the future and generally isn't healthy for the affected forest. Trees that are too small for the timber mill to process are scrapped into what's called a "slash pile" and burned; hence, there is not a valuable purpose in taking these trees that are too small to be processed. In many instances I've seen the USFS insist that the contracted timber company cut and take these trees that are too small to be processed because the USFS gets payment and funding based on the board feet the contractor takes from the forest. The contracted timber company is forced by the government to spend money and take these trees at a loss so that the USFS can get as much payment and funding from the timber sale they have offered to the public. If these trees were left to grow, not only would the USFS benefit from the increased funding and board feet due to future tree growth but the timber company (i.e. a segment of the economy) wouldn't have to needlessly suffer financial losses just so the USFS can receive funding in the present instead of in the future.

The USFS also has its own aviation inspection department that creates its own aviation standards and methods of inspection for civilian operators contracted by them. We already have an appropriate and capable government aviation entity to perform these functions in the Federal Aviation Administration (FAA). Many of the USFS and FAA standards are similar, but they are different enough that they conflict--leaving aviation companies to try and satisfy whichever standards they are trying to operate under at the time. Each of these USFS issues is relatively small on the government scale, but cumulatively issues like these, pooled together over the many agencies of the federal government, combine to be a substantial burden on our country. Shrewd, wise businessmen will confirm that it is in the managing of the details and the dollars, along with the millions, that paves the way to survival and success.

This is my observation and resulting assessment that comes from witnessing the effects of federal legislation in regards to our country's environment. Our country is made up of many different ecosystems and ecological regions that require handling, administration, and preservation based of the specific needs of that particular region. Because of this important fact, what is currently legislated at the federal level should be predominantly handled at the state level or regionally. You can't pass effective federal legislation in Washington D.C. that applies to all of the different ecosystems in the United States. There are too many differences from one region to another. For example, some forests need to be logged in a certain manner, such as clear-cut logging, that breaks up the soil and allows seedlings to germinate and reforest the area. Other regions suffer from the soil damage caused by these logging methods and consequently need to be logged using more environmentally- friendly methods so the area will reforest successfully. There are many other issues in our country that have regional concerns, such as water conservation, environmental habitat, and ecological concerns, etc., which require region-specific management and legislation. All of these could be better managed and represented by the states than by the federal government.

Another federal government experience includes my trying to obtain a patent. Man, what a complicated and expensive experience that is! If you could navigate the process yourself, without having to go into serious debt paying for a patent attorney, the United States would benefit economically by the additional influx of people willing to put forth their ideas for innovative, entrepreneurial endeavors. I, personally, have a number of inventions sketched out that I would love to pursue--if I didn't have to almost go bankrupt trying to bring these innovations to fruition. I have paid the attorney fees necessary to obtain a patent, and the costs were very burdensome and they have doubled in the last decade. I tried my second patent attempt myself by trying to solicit the help of the U.S. Patent and Trademark Office (USPTO), and while that office has made great improvements in the last decade, their process is not very user-friendly or forgiving if you don't understand the process and you happen to make a mistake. My point is that I personally have some valuable, proprietary, new services and merchandise that I would love to bring to the U.S. economy and marketplace but I can't get them there because of 1) the lack of funds, or 2) the requirements to obtain a patent are too complex and prohibitive. These innovations of mine are potential business ventures that would create jobs and pay taxes. Out of 307 million Americans, I doubt very seriously that I'm one case in 307 million. There are other Americans out there with probably more potential for success than I and are struggling to get their innovative ideas to market as well. I applied for my patent as a small business concern and, as such, the cost is reasonable but the process is too complex and hard to navigate.

I have gone through the Small Business Administration's (SBA) established process of trying to obtain funding and have used their suggested methods of successful business ventures. I spent six months writing a business plan as they recommended. I met with an SBA recommended venture capitalist--and if you're willing give them all the benefit of you being in business, then they will invest in themselves taking almost all the profits and you might be lucky enough to work for them. But hey, you get to be the boss! Well, I have a job and I don't need the title of "boss" to be happy. I live in America, I'm free, and that freedom means that I already am my own boss. My interest in small business is the satisfaction of personal accomplishment and investment in my own future for myself and my loved ones. I have used the SCORE organization and have learned from the experiences they share. At the end of the day, there are a lot of well-intentioned government people and agencies out there who are trying to help, but the reality of it is that, without money, you need a patent you can take to an investor to obtain funding. That's where the federal government has the ability to help entrepreneurs start new businesses and stimulate the economy with very little costs to the government and the taxpayer. We need to streamline and simplify the process of obtaining a patent so that these innovations can get to market. Let's streamline the process of innovations getting to the U.S. economy and market, for the benefit of the economy, the government, and society as a whole. Let's let our free markets live up to their potential. Let's help people realize their dreams and benefit as a country because of it. As a country, it's when we create an environment for opportunities that people get involved and risk trying to create the businesses that support economic growth and stability.

When I was in the military as a U.S. Army private, I remember lying out and organizing our company equipment for what used to be called an "Inspector General's (IG) inspection." We had laid out our GP medium tents, and I stood there, at parade rest, at the head of my tent as the Company Commander and the Inspector General strolled through. They stopped at my tent, and the Inspector General asked our commander, "Have you heard about the new dome tents we're getting to replace these?" Our commander replied, "No, sir." Then the IG asked, "Would you like some?" And our commander said, "yes, sir." Then the IG proceeded to take a knife out of his pocket and made a cut down the front of the tent I was taking care of. Then he said, "I don't believe this tent is serviceable, do you?" Our commander responded, "No, sir." Then they continued on down the row of tents and proceeded to cut up every tent we had.

Now, I understand that in a government bureaucracy like ours sometimes you have to work the system to get what you need--but we need to look at this type of problem and recognize that it exists. My commander should have been able to requisition the tents we needed, and sent the old tents to the National Guard, the Red Cross, the homeless in the warmer climates of our country, or somebody else who could have put them to good use. As a government, if we have to destroy and waste goods to justify replacing them or getting more, than we have a problem that needs to be fixed. This is a problem that cumulatively costs us more than we realize. We need to satisfy the reasonable needs of our government agencies in more responsive and proactive ways. We need to support their mission so that they can succeed for us. We need to increase or enforce the consequences of waste and abuse to more effectively deter this mentality. Management in government needs to fear the possibility that those witnessing their abuses could bring charges against them for their actions.

Not only should citizen witnesses to government abuse have the power to blow the whistle on their tax dollars being wasted, but they should receive an incentive for having taken the risk of pointing it out. Many times these witnesses are government employees that put themselves at risk in these situations. I don't care how good we think our "whistle blower" protection laws are; reality and the law can, many times, be very far apart and the risk for having spoken up and done the right thing for our country and our conscience should be recognized and rewarded. Let's put our money where our mouth is; we save money in the long run by stopping one more corner of abuse in our government. We save by the deterrence we create in the example and precedence we set and by the integrity we foster for our society to do the right thing, in all places and at all times. Let's get back to some of the old school principles that founded this country and made it so great. Integrity, honesty, patriotism, loyalty, sacrifice, service, character and commitment are hallmarks of many Americans throughout our history and we need to strengthen and support these qualities in our citizens for the betterment of our society. We will benefit from initiatives that reward and support these principles and codes of conduct.

As a civil service employee, I have seen fraud, waste, and abuse that are up in the millions of dollars and I am one employee at one building, at one location, in our country. I know I am not alone in having witnessed these frauds, wastes and abuses. I know this because almost everyone I talk to about this issue acknowledges the problem and agrees it exists. And again, that is just in my little corner of our country. There are literally millions of tax dollars that are thrown away, on a regular basis, in the name of inspection and inventory regulations. There are even more abuses that, I believe, get into the billions of dollars in regards to our governments contracting laws. Remember the news story and investigation over the government contract that paid $400 for a toilet seat? There are abuses of this type that range from the very small to the very large, with corresponding prices to match, in every agency in government. Not all items purchased by the government have inappropriate prices, but I've seen enough to believe that we could cut federal spending on commodities by at least 15%. Can you imagine what we could do if we could pay that much of our tax dollars towards our national debt? The savings in interest alone would be a huge boost for our situation economically.

CHAPTER THREE

POLITICAL THOUGHTS, IDEAS, AND SOLUTIONS

Our country has been suffering from the divisional, negative effects of two party politics since our third presidency. Some of the Founding Fathers wisely foresaw the distraction and deterrent this would be in the cause of things that are good for our country--that we would progressively be less willing to work together for the common good of our country and that party politics and special interests would pull us away from focusing on our country, first and foremost, in our deliberations. Now, these many years later, we have too many legislators that are focused on reelection and saving their political butts than there are willing to take the moral high ground for our country. Too often their focus is on how this legislation can help or hurt them personally. "Let the other guy (or gal) fall on the sword in the name of doing what's right. I have a reelection to win."

Our Founding Fathers had a vision of the people and the states having to be very vigilant in the oversight of our federal government and the protection of the governmental balances they set up. They also conceded and realized that a process for Constitutional improvements would have to be made to provide for things that they overlooked or didn't exist then and that might need to be dealt with in the future. Their thorough study of societies in history left the Founding Fathers with the realization that the trend in history of people and governments drawing power unto themselves was undeniable and needed to be protected against for our opportunity of freedoms and prosperity to survive. This chapter will span many different topics, but the overall theme will be the pursuit of preserving and improving, where possible, this country that we love for our children, our grandchildren, our families, ourselves, and for others willing to come here to contribute and love the freedoms and opportunities we enjoy.

I'm going to number these thoughts, ideas, and solutions in the hopes that they will be referenced, debated and discussed for the betterment of our country--should our country find them worthy of consideration.

1. Our form of representative government needs to be more direct to minimize the effects of the two-party politics that we suffer from and was feared by Washington, Jefferson, and others. Every bill or motion in Congress, in addition to being voted on by the seated members of the House of Representatives and the Senate, should be voted on by local representatives and governors in each state. This creates a greater check and balance of power between the federal government and the states, thereby reducing or checking the federal government's ability to misrepresent the states' interests.

The other side of that issue is that once federal legislation is passed, it should be supported by the states as was needed and called for by the Founding Fathers of our country. Just because a state didn't vote for a bill or motion doesn't mean it shouldn't uphold and support it--thereby giving credibility and integrity to our union.

The addition of a people's vote from the states would be a swing vote of conscience for both houses instead of those houses being corrupted by party politics and special interests. Instead of a two-party power struggle in Congress, the institution of a three-way balance of power will add representation to our legislative process and will shift the focus and power of Congress back towards the states and away from political party power in Washington. Federal politicians will be inclined to appeal to the people and the states, instead of operating through back room political deals and coercion in Washington. Transparency in our government will be greatly increased. We the people will be more intimately involved in the issues and the governing of our country.

2. Specifically, there should be state representation that more closely represents the local will of the people through voting by local representatives and governors that would vote on **ALL** congressional initiatives. These local representatives and governors would mirror, in representation, the current representation of the seated members elected to Congress.

In case of national emergencies, the seated Congress could pass emergency legislation to accommodate the nation through national crises without the representation of the local representatives and governors. All local representation must be excluded wholly, if unable to satisfy congressional requirements for a quorum of representation and that quorum could only be excluded in case of national emergencies or lack of communication. The communication method for each local representative and governor should be functionally tested for serviceability and recorded locally to validate proper accounting of the vote in Congress through the published voting record in Congress.

The combined congressional representation would expand from 538 members to 1020 members. The local representatives and governors should be the only congressional members to vote on issues of the seated members' congressional pay, entitlements and privileges. Having local, congressional representation, on the ground in each state, will hopefully reduce and minimize the disconnect that we currently experience between legislation from Washington D.C. and what's needed by the states abroad. Because of the physical separation between members of Congress these satellite members will be more prone to be objective and vote based on the merits of the proposed legislation and the dictates of conscience instead of peer pressure and persuasion by seated members. If you've ever read about the role of a party whip in Congress, the whole role and notion of coercing votes sounds scandalous and corrupt. Seated members of Congress, their staff or their representatives, should be prohibited, by law, from soliciting and persuading the vote of local representatives and governors. Local representatives and governors can seek additional information from members of Congress but seated members should be sequestered from contacting them about the issues or their vote.

Local representatives and governors should have a brief review period of an established time to review the debate by the seated congressional members on the issues up for vote and to vote within a prescribed time frame. The time frame should be long enough to digest a synopsis version of what is proposed by Congress but short enough to keep a reasonable flow of productivity in Congress. The time frame should be debated and kept flexible to revision so that we can adjust and benefit from our experience of using such a system. Current seated members of Congress might complain that these constitutional amendments would slow down Congress' ability to pass legislation, which will be functionally true. But here's the question: is it the quantity or the quality of legislation that we are seeking from our Congress? Consider the profound effects that these legislative initiatives have on the lives of our fellow countrymen and our country. I say that it is quality legislation that we stand in need of from our Congress--legislation that has local, state, and regional support.

Unfortunately, we currently have a legislative body that is crippled by party politics. If we don't devise a means of overcoming this form of corruption, our country will continue to spiral downward-- away from integrity and virtue-- until it no longer represents the worthy aspirations of our country and its people. Creating a fair and representative swing vote of the states (people), although it will still be susceptible to party politics, will further divide the balance of power in our government between federal and state, giving back more representative power to the states and the people. The Constitution is full of admonitions for the states to keep vigilant watch over the federal government to protect against the usurpation of governmental power away from the states. Doesn't it make sense that the only effective way to do that is to have a local state representative influencing that branch of government?

3. These local representatives could be provided in the form of each state's legislative bodies and would not receive federal compensation for their vote. We're already paying them to represent our individual states; we would just be expanding their influence and opportunity to represent us. The states would still only have the ratio and number of representative votes as currently established by federal

census. These local representatives should be elected by their state's legislative peers to represent their state and should report their federal House of Representative deliberations and decisions to their state legislature at least once a month.

Local representatives shall not be eligible to again hold that position if their district representatives elected to that position hold that position one time more than other voting districts and/or their legislative peers. This provision will inhibit nepotism and aristocracy from among those representatives and/or districts chosen as local representatives and will ensure that the least among our state representatives will not be left behind in the privilege and opportunity to represent their constituents at a federal level. This way all Americans will eventually be represented at the federal level by a local representative from their district.

These local representatives would vote on all federal House of Representative bills or motions that come before that body. These local representatives could vote only and could not write or initiate legislation in Congress. Every ten years the sitting local representatives would represent their state in a combined meeting with the seated members of Congress in Washington D.C. during the last congressional session of the census year. They could only initiate legislation in regards to congressional rules that affect their role and ability to represent the people-- kind of a performance survey/process improvement session. These local representative sponsored bills would be voted on by both local and seated members. The local representative bills would be heard every decade as the first order of business during the last congressional session of the federal census year. All initiatives brought by the local representatives would be heard and voted on before normal congressional business moves forward for that session.

The government census every decade would determine representation, as it does currently. The combined number of members of the House of Representatives would be 435 seated representatives and 435 local representatives. The current rules governing a quorum and the percentage or fractional amount required to pass legislation by that body would still apply.

4. Every governor of every state should have one vote in the U.S. Senate on all congressional initiatives that come before that body. These governors would not receive federal compensation for their vote; we're already paying them to represent our individual states. We would just be expanding their influence and opportunity to represent us. These executives of each state, being more aware of the state's ability to implement the legislation that comes

before Congress, should have the ability to protect their state's interest through their vote on legislation that comes before Congress. The Senate, as a legislative body, will benefit from the local knowledge, experience and concerns that these governors have for their states.

The governors could vote only and could not write or initiate legislation in Congress. Governors who are serving at the time of the census year should be able to participate in a combined meeting with Congress during the last congressional session of the federal census year every decade. They could only initiate legislation in regards to congressional rules that affect their role and ability to represent the people in an effort to improve the representation and the will of the people. The governors would be heard as the second order of business during the last congressional session of the census year. All initiatives brought by the governors shall be heard and voted on before normal congressional business moves forward for that session.

The combined number of U.S. Senators would be increased to 150 members: 100 Senators and 50 governors. The current rules governing a quorum and the percentage or fractional amount required to pass legislation by that body would still apply.

5. Upon the retirement or death of the next U.S. Supreme Court justice, the vacant position should be filled by the collective voice and vote of every respective state attorney general with the United States Attorney General voting in case of a tie among the states to produce the nation's collective Supreme Court vote on all decisions regarding the judiciary branch of our government. Should there not be a quorum (75%) of the state attorney general's available to legitimize their vote, then the United States Attorney General would fill in as the people's vote until a quorum of representation is reestablished among the states. Likewise, in the case of the loss of communications with the state attorney general's and/or national emergencies requiring expedient decisions by the United States Supreme Court, the United States Attorney General would vote to represent the people until such time as timely communications have been reestablished and/or the national emergency has passed.

Because of this representative responsibility being placed upon the position of the United States Attorney General, that position should be an elected position whose votes are cast by a quorum of the state attorneys general with the President of the United States casting the deciding vote in the case of a tie.

An alternate and probably better method of adding the people's representation to our legislative branch of government would be to have the United States Attorney General be a member of the Supreme Court after having been elected by a quorum of the states attorneys generals. Either way, it's more representative of the will of the people than we have currently. Like our legislative branch, the judiciary branch of our government has also succumbed to the weaknesses of two-party motivations and allegiances, whether it be liberal or conservative, democrat or republican, constitutional preference or judiciary activism, etc. The majority rule of society and the people's representation on these important issues has been diminished and needs to be reestablished to more fully represent the will of the people. One vote for the people and the states, against eight appointed votes by the federal government and the controlling political parties, is not too much representation to ask for. Again, I say we stand in need of a swing vote of conscience from the people in our government processes to break up our government's tendency to obtain power unto itself and to return power back to the people where it belongs. This one vote will provide much needed representation for the states that have to enact, fulfill, and live by the decisions and laws handed down by our judicial branch of government. This one vote will serve as a potential tie-breaking vote that will help protect our freedoms by providing opposition to decisions that solely represent federal mandates, political and activist parties, or special interest initiatives.

The balance of power in our judicial branch of government, slightly shifting from the federal government towards the people and the states, is completely in line with the spirit of freedom written into the original version of our constitution. The constitution is full of admonitions for the states to keep vigilant watch over the federal government to protect against the usurpation of governmental power away from the people. Doesn't it make sense that the only effective way to do that is to have state representation in that branch of government?

6. A constitutional convention should be convened every 300 years. The beginning of this convention should begin with a review of and vote on those unalienable rights and parts of our government that we collectively choose to protect and take off the table for consideration. Once we have collectively addressed our fears and concerns with the constitutional convention process, and those fears and concerns have been protected through state ratification, we should then move forward to promote changes for the good of our country as a whole. Any changes would still have to stand up to the state ratification process, as they do currently, or things would remain as they are.

This process sounds tedious and redundant, but for something that has the potential to make profound changes to our government and our lives the process should be undertaken with great caution and care. We must never forget that the adversary for good, whether you believe that to be the depravity and weakness of man or any other entity, will be present and looking for opportunities to capitalize and manipulate this process. It will be through thorough, careful consideration, reflection, and prayer that those depraved influences and weaknesses will be made evident and the opposing goodness in what we consider will be confirmed. As long as we properly protect ourselves in this process, only good, up-to-date changes should come from it.

7. The government should provide an annual report-- available online and posted as a hardcopy synopsis at all U.S. Post Offices--that lists all of the issues heard by the government for the year and the voting record of all our federally elected and appointed officials (primarily the president, senators, representatives, and Supreme Court judges). As a society, we can no longer afford to be uninformed about the details of our government. We shouldn't trust that a supposedly unbiased media will provide the information we need to cast an informed vote. Our freedoms are at risk when we are uninformed as a society. An accounting of our government needs to be provided, by the government, as a protection of our freedoms and from the corruption of our government. The importance of this being provided by a reliable government entity, such as the Government Accounting Office or any other appropriate, unbiased, non-partisan, government entity, cannot be overemphasized.

8. As a country, we should never borrow more than 90% of our annual Gross Domestic Product (GDP), and if we are, than we are living way beyond our means. We don't have the right to burden our posterity with debt we've created and inhibit their freedom of choice. It's kind of hypocritical from a country that supports freedom of choice around the world but not for our own children at home.

The Founding Fathers debated the issue of passing on debt to our posterity and they did not support the practice. They felt that each generation should support and pay the debt they created and that the national debt should never extend beyond what that generation could pay off. Our country has a long history of debt and has rarely been found to not be in debt. Given the track record of our government and politicians, we should pass a law limiting the damage that can be done to our country through the accumulation of debt. Are we comfortable with our government having the power to bankrupt our country, our lives, and our ability to work and survive by placing a financial lien against these values of worth to foreign and domestic investors? Are we comfortable with our government having the power to barter away our country and our freedoms? I think we need to set some prudent limits on the damage that can be done. We need to protect the American people, our way of life, and our society.

9. Certain business segments of society, deemed by society to be fundamental and critical to the welfare and prosperity of society, could be eligible for the government to enter into and participate in the free market process of that particular

business segment for the purpose of stabilizing the cost and availability of that declared need by society. The government-run business entity would have to adhere to the laws of the land as do non-government business entities. The appropriate taxes levied and the profits made by the government business entity would be applied to the national debt to reduce the national tax requirement. The maximum percentage of profit that the government business entity would be entitled to make would be set by the people via Congress. The profit margin should be high enough to sustain the business segment in the marketplace, but low enough to reduce the burden on society for the declared need that is deemed essential and critical. The business segments of society I feel that should be considered for government participation in the free market process are pharmaceuticals, petroleum products, higher education, hospitals, and health insurance--in that order. If the government believes in the free market process, why wouldn't it participate in and support it as a member of the free market process? If some government agencies are involved in the free market process, congress might better understand, as a recipient of its own legislation, which laws stimulate, which ones deter and those that should be required in regards to our free market economy. Hypothetical scenarios are okay, but there's nothing like physically experiencing the reality of things to obtain true understanding.

- Pharmaceuticals should be the first business segment that the government should participate with in the free market process. Pharmaceuticals have a high impact on the quality of life, physically and economically, for many in society. Thus, the sustained need and/or demand by society are relatively high. The employee requirement is comparatively low (machinery and equipment do a lot of the work). The return on investment is relatively high. The startup costs are low, compared to the other business segments. Substantial savings could be realized by the government and society through our military pharmaceutical requirements for active duty members and retirees. The capacity for the government to respond to national epidemics, biological attacks, or any other similar national threats requiring a reliable source of pharmaceuticals would be a source of national protection and could be considered a national health and security interest.

- Petroleum products are necessary for our national defense and the health of our economy until such time as science and innovation causes them to be obsolete or less required by our economy. There are many benefits of the government competing in this business sector, including having the internal capacity to convert strategic oil reserves into fuel to use for the defense of our interest, and to stabilize the price of petroleum products for the health of the economy and to deter price gouging of the American consumer through stabilizing, free market competition.

- Many able and creative minds in this country do not reach their potential due to their lack of funds, their personal circumstances, and the cost of many higher education institutions. As the people of this country are either unable or unwilling to reach their potential, so is the country as a whole not able or willing to reach its potential. This is one recommendation for which there are many possible solutions. Unfortunately, there is not an upfront financial benefit in addressing the educational aspirations of our country and this would be a short-term financial burden and investment. Our country will benefit more in taxes being paid from a higher earning, more educationally advanced work force, but the returns are into the future and they are not a short-term benefit. Consider the creation of a U.S. Military Education Reserves, an entity which would create opportunity for educational, physical, and personal growth to the benefit of society and the country. Candidates would go through preliminary, basic training to prepare them for the rigors and work ethic necessary to succeed in their goals of educational, physical, and personal growth. All contentious objectors or those unwilling to harm others would be welcome. Classes would be available via the Internet or traditional classroom presentation, and would be monitored and assisted by military cadre who would conduct and direct the students as required. Local schools and/or post offices could be used or expanded as necessary to facilitate classes. Those students that meet and pass the requirements of this general education and entry phase could move on to state or regional military academies for continued growth in specific fields of study. Reserve drills could be required occasionally. This program would realistically be better managed by the states with shared financial support coming from the federal government, so long as the states meet or follow program guidelines. This educational, physical, and personal growth opportunity would be available to everyone with personal cost fluctuating based on personal income for adults more than 25 years of age and parental income for those less than 25 years of age. Emancipation status and/or financial assistance could be applied for by potential students whose parents are unwilling or unable to help their children's educational aspirations, but those parents would lose their entitlement to claim that child as a dependent for tax purposes if that child received emancipation status. Time in the U.S. Military Education Reserves could count as time in government service after successful completion of a bachelor's degree or higher degree in the U.S. Military Education Reserves Academy and upon entry into the armed services.

10.Any state lands to be sold should first be offered to the federal government to give the government the opportunity to secure those lands for the people and our country. The American people deserve the opportunity to enjoy and experience these lands for themselves and their posterity. Their tax dollars are given in support of their country and their state, and it is reasonable to expect that the elected stewards of their public land resources should not take away their access to these lands through mismanagement and/or their sale to private entities. Voter approval should be required to sell state and national lands, and not the approval of a misguided elected official. A vote for a public official should not automatically give that official the authority to take away our public lands by any means. Only those lands deemed unsafe or preserved should be restricted from public use. The government and the states can establish guidelines for public use of public lands, but citizens willing to comply with these requirements should be allowed access to their public resources. Many lands are regularly being bought by private entities that in turn restrict access to these once public natural resources. Many times, this means the use and enjoyment of these lands is limited to only those who have the financial means to pay for access. It is not in our interest to sell our country to private or foreign interest. I believe it is in the interest of the common citizens of our country to preserve the condition of and the opportunity for access to these natural resources.

11. Aristocracy and corruption exists in many places in our government in the form of nepotism. There are many people in government that, as they rise in power and status, give preferential treatment, status, and position to benefit their family and friends beneath themselves and essentially create an influential base of support for themselves and their careers. Family and friends are shuffled and moved around between organizations, so as not to violate our laws regarding nepotism. Because our laws regarding nepotism have a defined area and specific range of focus in determining what nepotism is, there is opportunity for corrupt people within government to move their unethical and corrupt choices, their nepotism, just outside the definition of the law so as to not be in violation. They're playing the system, with the justification that they didn't violate the definition of the law, while the government turns a blind eye. This problem and plague of governmental corruption can be easily seen and proven through the documented movement of personnel just outside the legal definition of nepotism. The opportunity and selection for government service should be based on a person's knowledge, skills and abilities--not by their family relations,

religion, lack of religion, looks, color, gender, nationality, or in being one of the "good ole boys," or part of the chosen aristocracy of that government entity. The fact that most people agree and are aware that this exists is circumstantial proof of its existence. A federal inquiry, with a little more than mild effort, could very easily provide physical proof of this form of corruption in our government. To restore credibility, trust and confidence of the American people in our government, nepotism needs to be stopped.

12.Every item or service contracted to the government should come with complete detailed, fabrication, process, and production plans so that the government isn't held hostage to exorbitant high prices, fraud, waste, abuse and non-performance. If under this proposal our government obtained such plans, they should be secured and archived and the government should continue to observe the contractors' proprietary rights until such time that those proprietary rights and privileges have expired. At that time, the government has every right to make this information public to share that opportunity with our free market system and to thereby benefit from the competition within the market, the corresponding reduction in cost, and from the product availability. The contractor to the government should have every reasonable opportunity to fulfill the terms of their contract, but should they be unable to perform their contracted service, then the federal government should not be held hostage by the contractors' inability to produce what was contracted and claimed. Under this scenario of non-performance, the government should be entitled to offer the contract to another entity-- with the restriction of non-disclosure of proprietary information by the new entity-- and that the new performing entity could not benefit financially outside of the specific contract which entitled them to the proprietary information released to them by the government. There are numerous government contracts out there that price gouge the government and they have no recourse other than to pay these exorbitant high prices because the government doesn't have the proprietary information available to offer these opportunities to other entities. Many times these commodities, that have proprietary exclusions to them, have patents that expired decades ago but the government still has to pay exorbitant high prices because they don't have the information necessary to produce it themselves or have others produce it for them. These exclusive vendors aren't about to give up their market advantage and information. Who can blame them? Why would they give up a market advantage like that? The duration of proprietary rights and privileges were established to give incentive and opportunity for a substantial return and to give exclusiveness in the marketplace for having taken the risk of bringing their innovations to market and society.

Our government cannot afford to be held hostage to exorbitant high prices and non-performance indefinitely. That was not the intent when the government extended these proprietary rights and privileges to these entities and the government needs to pass contracting laws to protect themselves from these kinds of abuses. The solution is a simple one--if you want a government contract of any kind, you must provide full disclosure of drawings, processes, and information necessary to fulfill all aspects of the product or service contained within that contract. Without it, you're not eligible for the offered government contract. The government can reverse engineer what is needed if they have to. We will save money in the long run. This process will stimulate engineering utilization in our country that could produce windfall businesses while saving our country billions of dollars every year! As a government, we are paying high prices for things that, in some cases, were developed in the 1960's. These companies have received substantial return on their investment decades ago and are still doing so today at our economic expense and health. Enough is enough--we cannot support excesses like these any longer. We're at the threshold of what we can financially bear as a country.

13.We need to incorporate, within our government and constitution, the ability to benefit from the experience gained by presidents and Supreme Court justices. The gleaning of the value of the experiences from the proposed local representatives and governors has already been discussed, and seated members of Congress already have the opportunity and privilege to improve our government and constitution through the positions they hold in that branch of government. Each retired president and Supreme Court justice should have the opportunity to submit one bill to Congress, for deliberations by that body after their tenure, so that as a country we can benefit from the experience and knowledge they've gained while in our service. Although these bills need not be written in the census year, it makes sense for these bills to be submitted during the census year at the same time as was previously suggested in regards to local representatives and governors, = consolidating these initiatives into one session of Congress.

The legislative branch of our government does not have the perspective, knowledge, and experience that come from having served in those capacities and because of this could be totally unaware of some of the considerations and challenges of serving in the other two branches of our government. The opportunity to address these challenges or issues, in the best interest of our country and government, could be easily overlooked. Currently there is not an effective way of addressing oversights in our form of government or the functional needs of the other two branches except through the opposing legislative branch which is biased to retain power unto itself and not extend it. This is another example for the need of state influence through local representatives and governors. The legislative branch would still have to deliberate and vote on any such bill allowing for the opportunity to benefit from the lessons learned by those who have served our country for extended periods of time. I believe these experienced public servants could provide valuable information, ideas, and improvements to the branch of government that they served in, to the benefit of our form of government and our country. Our leaders are some of the brightest minds in our country. For us to overlook this potentially valuable source of information and ideas is a serious oversight.

14. Many of us have heard the term "trickle-down economics" as a description of the economic platform generally promoted by the Republican Party. This term has sometimes been used negatively by the Democratic Party to mock and demean the Republican Party's position on economic policy. The term "trickle-down economics" is generally used to describe the philosophy that as the government will allow business and the economy to operate unimpeded, then business and the economy will tend to prosper and that prosperity will trickle down through society to the benefit of all. There is truth in this philosophy and its effects, but the trickle down effects can be limited by the

integrity and generosity of the recipients at the top of this pyramid-type economic structure. If the business entities at the top of this structure choose to retain their profits unto themselves, instead of investing in expansion and growth, then the economy stagnates and the prosperity that could be trickled down from the top of this structure is less than it could or ethically should be in the interest of society and the economy.

Another economic term we have heard of is "welfare economics" as a description of the economic platform generally promoted by the Democratic Party. This term has likewise been used negatively by the Republican Party to mock and demean the Democratic Party's position on economic policy. The term "welfare economics" is generally used to describe the philosophy of taxing and regulating business, the economy and society to ensure prosperity is distributed throughout society through social and welfare programs. The problem with this philosophy is that while "trickle-down economics" tends to put people to work, "welfare economics" has relatively no requirement for work for that segment of society who receives the prosperity that is distributed by these government programs. When these programs create sustained support, they tend to create dependency. These programs struggle to be cost effective at redistributing prosperity to society because they are not exposed to the competition and motivation required by our free market system to survive. Their survival is guaranteed by the tax payer, regardless of how effective they are. These programs are funded with less regard for their competiveness and effectiveness but more for their political value between receiving constituents and their politicians. All of this means that the common citizen receives far less prosperity than was intended or is possible by other, more effective means. Morally, we have an obligation to help the poor and needy with just enough for them to help themselves--but not for so much and for so long as to handicap them with dependency. Listen to these inspired words on this subject by Benjamin Franklin:

"To relieve the misfortunes of our fellow creatures is concurring with Deity; it is godlike; but, if we provide encouragement for laziness, and supports for folly, may we not be found fighting against the order of God and Nature, which perhaps has appointed want and misery as the proper punishments for, and cautions against, as well as necessary consequences of, idleness and extravagance? Whenever we attempt to amend the scheme of Providence, and to interfere with the government of the world, we had need be very circumspect, lest we do more harm than good."

Again, while it's in the interest of society to help those in need, it is corrosive to society to go beyond helping with temporary problems into creating dependency. Those with proven, long-term disabilities should be supported and excluded from contributing beyond their capacities, but should contribute within their capacity to do so.

There are numerous ways of stimulating and supporting the welfare of those in temporary need other than social programs. One idea is eliminating frivolous tax write-offs for businesses and society and to expand the tax credits available to those entities for charitable contributions. Another idea is government sponsored TV ads through PBS stations to advertise for qualified charities in need. As a nation, when we individually support charitable contributions, not only are we blessed with the personal joy of giving but we become attached and involved in the service of our fellow Americans, which can bind and unify us as a country. As we receive service personally, we will in turn be motivated and inspired to serve others out of appreciation. Service fosters service. How many of us feel emotionally attached towards our fellow Americans when we pay taxes that go towards welfare and social programs? Instead of feeling bound and unified to our fellow Americans, many feel frustrated and violated because they didn't have a choice in their contribution. When we serve and contribute to the benefit of others, we become bound by concern and commitment to those we serve. Our unity as a nation is increased when we serve each other.

There are a few justified reasons for the government to intervene into business and the economy, in the interest of society as a whole, but these reasons generally are rare and are only justified when it can be proven that the intervention will have a sustained benefit to society. It is not in the best interest of society for government to chase the normal and justified corrections in the economy and marketplace. To do so will just delay the necessary, market-driven corrections that will ultimately happen anyway. Postponement of these corrections can sometimes require even bigger and more painful corrections than would have been required if the market had been left alone to correct itself. Government intervention can sometimes make things worse, depending upon the market's reaction to the intervention. Our free market system was designed by our Founding Fathers to give society the power to support those businesses, their products and services that they like, by exercising freedom of choice and their vote of approval through their dollars spent in support of those businesses. The dollars we spend are casting a vote of approval towards those businesses that we support. Successful businesses, in a truly free market system, naturally have the financial support of society. Subsidies, bail outs, and bankruptcies are governmental support of business in spite of society's choice and/or they are government's remission and assumption of failed business practices. Both of these practices saddle society with a burden they did not choose and are morally and ethically wrong.

Our Founding Fathers believed in an economic philosophy found in a book famous for its time, written and published in 1776 by Adam Smith entitled *The Wealth of Nations*. A good description of this economic philosophy would be to call it "prosperity economics" because it focuses on the prosperity of society as its goal and purpose. By the end of the nineteenth century, this economic philosophy was beginning to give Americans the highest standard of living in the world. With less than 6 percent of the earth's population, Americans were producing more than half of all goods produced worldwide. This was made possible because our constitution allowed four vital principles contained in *The Wealth of Nations*. These fundamental economic principles and freedoms are:

1. The freedom to **try**
2. The freedom to **buy**
3. The freedom to **sell**
4. The freedom to **fail**

These once constitutionally guaranteed freedoms emphasize that one of the greatest enemies to a free market economy is illegitimate government intervention. In a true, free market economy, there are generally only four conditions where governmental intervention is legitimate:

1. To prevent force (criminal invasion of the market)
2. To prevent fraud (invasion of the market through deception)

3. To prevent monopoly of the market (destruction of competitive free trade)
4. To prevent debauchery (exploitation of vices detrimental to the community, such as gambling, drugs, prostitution, pornography, etc.)][3]

The fourth reason for governmental intervention should be in line with the will of the majority of society and should be applied or repealed according to the will and support of the people. Currently, some of these vices are allowed in segregated settings such as in Nevada, Atlantic City, and in Native American casinos, etc.

The underlying principle and theme of "prosperity economics" is that a successful free market system is one that has free, unbiased competition in the marketplace, which eventually produces products that are abundant and cheap. This promotes and increases our standard of living and prosperity, while maximizing healthy economic capacity throughout society. It's when there is a lack of healthy competition in the market that product prices soar beyond normal levels and these artificially high prices put a financial strain on society. When the profits of our free market system are concentrated into just a few, instead of being spread across the many, the amount of jobs and growth of the economy are tied to the financial decisions of those few and what they decide to do with their profits. Let's face it-- profits pay for our prosperity.

When healthy competition exists in the marketplace, there are just enough profits to survive with modest security in the market. Your security becomes more tied to customer service and satisfaction than your exclusive position in the market. Healthy market competition spreads profits over many market entities, creating jobs and growth with those profits instead of creating a comfortable nest egg and financial position for those few who aren't burdened with competitive market pressures.

I believe that in those business segments deemed by society to be critical and essential, the government is justified in participating in the free market process to restore healthy competition back to the marketplace. Although free, fair competition as a means of market price control isn't generally promoted by our government, I believe it is the only method of price control that is in line with the freedoms created by our constitution and the economic freedoms described in the book *The Wealth of Nations*.

When governments place regulatory limitations on the market, the market's potential is diminished and society's prosperity is diminished as well. We need to restore economic policy that is focused on what is good for the majority, while providing for the needs of the few in a limited, targeted way to create the opportunity for the independence that the majority of society is enjoying. Free, united, and service toward each other are backbone principles of "prosperity economics."

While "trickle-down economics" restrains government and promotes the freedoms required for a successful free marketplace, this philosophy overlooks the tendency of the financial aristocracy in our country to draw wealth unto itself first and foremost. Taking financial risk or investment of wealth into growth, jobs creation and economic stability usually comes second. What the financial upper class of this country isn't acknowledging and realizing is that stabilizing the economy reduces their risk and stabilizes their prosperity.

"Welfare economics" subsidizes so many different levels of society from individuals to businesses that it creates unfair advantages in society and the marketplace. For some business segments, "welfare economics" replaces fair trade and healthy competition with unfair advantages--both financially and regulatory. This causes free market interest to withdraw from those business segments, leaving them barren from competition and further solidifying the need to be subsidized. This, in turn, can give Congress false justification to continue subsidies to save that business segment of the market, when fair competition is what is truly required for interested parties to invest. Who wants to invest and try to compete against unfair government subsidies? I wouldn't have anything to do with that business segment, either. The problems created by subsidies justify more subsidies and progressively makes the problem worse. Before you know it, you have government backed business with no competition and no need to be productive or effective to survive. As a business, you can do whatever the tax payer is willing to bear with a diminished concern about effectiveness, frugality, or competition.

Individual, justified, and temporary welfare has been previously discussed and should be supported when its goal is short-term support to enable personal independence not government dependence.

We prospered more than any nation on earth in our first century by following the principles of "prosperity economics." The economic roller coaster ride we've experienced since then, while we've dabbled in Marxist and progressive economic philosophies, have brought us to a state where today we run the real risk of economic failure and collapse. In the wake of such a failure, the supporters of these imported economic philosophies will say that we failed because we were caught between capitalism and communism. They argue that for the good of all, we need to stop holding back and progress toward "progressive economics" i.e. communism or a new world order. To that notion I say, "Hello, look around! It's not working for anybody else who is free." Communism can only succeed through tyranny and undercutting a free market or by global domination under one dictatorship or "new world order," if you want to call it that. I don't know about you, but I'm not giving up my freedoms to try it.

That leaves us with the realization that patriotic Americans will always insist that we remain a free nation. A free nation requires a free market system that provides the freedom to succeed without illegitimate government intervention. Because we are a nation of freedoms, we will always need a free market system. We need to quit dabbling in things that are contrary to freedom--like the redistribution of wealth--and commit ourselves to freedom in all aspects of our country.

Charity and welfare that is forced or taxed does not bind us together as a nation and creates greater economic class divisions.

We need to reestablish the principles of "prosperity economics" that this country was founded on so that individuals and businesses are again free from illegitimate government control and given the chance to prosper and live up to their potential. It's when society is healthy economically that the lower class has the greatest potential to rise up from where they are. The potential charitable services and support, which can come through a healthy middle class, can reach far more people in the community than the government or the rich can effectively provide. We know where those in need live and what their needs are because they are our neighbors. To modify a quote from John F. Kennedy: "Ask not what [the government or the rich] can do for you, but ask what you can do for [yourself and your neighbor]." Now that's the spirit America was founded upon! If we will do that, we will prosper

15.The issue of presidential powers in regards to being commander-in-chief of our Armed Forces should be discussed. To give a little background, it was always the intent of our Founding Fathers that the power to conduct war or any other hostile military action should come through support of the people by their elected representatives in Congress. It was also the Founding Fathers' view that once such a military declaration was made, then the president, as commander-in-chief, should have full control of the Armed Forces to fulfill the mission, with the responsiveness, covertness, and the decisiveness required to protect our troops and to succeed.

The need for the commander-in-chief to have the flexibility to respond quickly in the face of dire situations involving our national interest was addressed and provided for in the War Powers Act of 1973. This power to respond quickly was meant to be temporary in nature and was meant to depend upon congressional support for hostile military actions to continue on a long-term basis.

The President of The United States having sole control of our Armed Forces dates back to our founding and has always been a given--yet it is a power I wish to create national discussion about. I understand why the Founding Fathers, especially Washington, insisted on the commander-in-chief being a citizen of the people and not an acting member of the military. History has plenty of examples of military commanders rising to military dictatorship over societies. I also understand that requiring others to be present to communicate and make decisions during our Founding Fathers' era wasn't always very practical. Congress, even then, could be very indecisive and communications were slow, creating a logistical handicap to the notion of more than one person making quick decisions. But today, we have communications capabilities that our Founding Fathers could not have foreseen, which enable us to communicate anytime, anywhere.

My question is this: could the role of commander-in-chief be modified to incorporate the experience of the Joint Chief of Staff Commander without taking away the people's control of our military through our elected representatives? We have had many presidents in our history that have had no military experience and even the ones that have had military experience usually haven't had the depth of experience that our career military commanders have. I picture our president, with little to no military experience, explaining military strategy to a career military general with thirty to forty years of experience. Now, something sounds wrong with this picture! Most, if not all, of our high-ranking military commanders have studied in depth and/or have experienced military history, strategy and operations. The fact that our military decisions can be made excluding the invaluable knowledge of our military commanders isn't very prudent and needs to be discussed.

Consider an arrangement where military decisions are made by a committee consisting of the President of the United States, the Senate Majority Leader, the Speaker of the House, the Secretary of Defense, and the Joint Chiefs of Staff Commander. The people's representation would still have the majority, four to one, due to the Secretary of Defense being appointed by the president, but our military experience would be represented in our military decisions. A smart president would rely on the experience of his or her military commanders, but as things are now these decisions can be made exclusively by the president in spite of what is recommended. I believe that a few heads are better than one, and together, a full committee could make more thorough decisions and be less prone to oversights and/or mistakes. Each member of the "Commander-in-Chief Committee" could be mandated to respond to a "decision call" by the president within a prescribed time frame. If necessary, the president would still have the authority to command and commit the Armed Forces. Also, any risk involving disclosure of military plans through unsecured communications could be assessed by the president and enable them to act alone as he or she believes is in the best interest of the country. The "Commander-in-Chief Committee" would be sequestered, as necessary, to protect our troops and our interest. Living in the communication age, I doubt this will happen very often or for long periods of time. The presence of others being involved in our military decisions can check and possibly prevent decisions from being made that are not sound or in the best interest of our country. The representatives of the people (Congress) should mandate what our military missions are, but the experience of our military commanders should influence how best to accomplish those missions. Instead of having to just notify the Speaker of the House as we currently do, the Speaker of the House would be part of the decision on when and how to commit military force. Instead of having to simply notify and consult the Joint Chief of Staff Commander, the commander would be part of the decision process on how and when to commit military force. I'm sure he is now, but legally it is a courtesy. The fundamental idea of including, by mandate of law, the experience of our military commanders in our military decisions needs to be debated and implemented so long as it doesn't comprise the people's control of our military. It's not wise or realistic to expect a president, with little or no military background, to make sound military decisions in our behalf.

16.Another military observation and concern I have is that we don't fully utilize our technological capabilities to our advantage. Here are a few thoughts.

a) I know of engineering firms that are capable of manufacturing and installing protective armor that could greatly increase the survivability of vehicles exposed to Improvised Explosive Devise (IED) blasts. I've heard news reports of protective armor being available for Humvees, but that they were not being fielded fast enough to meet the demand. Really? We're in such a big hurry to accomplish the mission that casualties are an acceptable risk? If there are technical advantages out there that can save the lives of our soldiers, and we're not fielding those advantages with all the ability that this great country is capable of, then shame on us.

b) I've seen video footage of ground field commanders using the support of unmanned aerial drones to locate, evaluate, and engage, with ordinance and firepower, the enemies of our soldiers. The fact that every field commander doesn't have this valuable tool at his disposal means that in some cases unnecessary risk is taken on by our soldiers. I realize that there is not a replacement for the courage and ingenuity of the American soldier and that some things can only be done by this caliber of weapon. But for those instances where the terrain or situation would allow a drone to take that risk for our soldiers, if we don't provide it for them then shame on us.

c) Urban warfare creates some of the most dangerous combat situations that can be found. Cover for the enemy is everywhere. In my opinion, if units went into these environments with intimidating firepower and the protective cover that can be provided by tanks and armored fighting vehicles, such as a Bradley fighting vehicle or equivalent, they would be less vulnerable to attack. If we don't have enough of these available, then we need to get what our soldiers need, on the ground, ASAP to maximize their safety. A fast, rear-entry, armored personnel carrier with a strong main gun and multiple machine guns on each side, complete with day or night scope sights feeding an internal monitor sounds futuristic but is well within our capability to produce. I'm willing to bet we have a few experienced video gamers in our military that would love to pull the trigger on something like that. We need to use whatever protects us and gives us an advantage.

d) If I've heard of helicopter mine sweepers in the Navy, why haven't I heard of armored IED sweepers leading our military convoys? If we are in too big of a hurry to use our technological abilities to our advantage, then we're not being very smart and our priorities need to be readjusted.

e) Our military is capable of creating operational headquarters and airfields anywhere in the world. Why did we set up operations in Bagdad, or similar areas, surrounded by urban cover for terrorists to launch attacks from? We could have set up in locations with no perimeter cover so that our enemies would have had to cross under the unimpeded surveillance of our perimeter guards. I remember hearing about different colored zones in Bagdad and seeing how much cover surrounded these zones and thinking that nothing looked safe about that situation. I'm sure there are tactical considerations I'm not aware of, but if the decision was a matter of convenience for facilities then shame on us for taking on unneeded risk just to take the logistical "easy way out." If nothing else, we should have bulldozed a wide, barren perimeter around wherever we wanted to stay and then installed a posted minefield. That might sound harsh to some, but our troops deserve the most effective protection and safe zone that we can provide.

17.Let's recognize that our national debt has a huge impact on our need to be taxed. Without real debt reduction, any talk about tax cuts puts off our responsibility to pay our debts into the future. Tax cuts are always popular in an election year. While tax cuts can stimulate the economy, at some point we have to deal with our debt or eventually it will overrun us and consume more than can be paid through taxes. We will then either have to bankrupt the world or be servants to our debt. Either way, our economic freedoms will have been compromised. We are all aware of how complex and burdensome our tax laws have become. It's obvious that we need to simplify our tax system. To simplify our tax laws, stimulate the economy and create job growth, I recommend the following:

In a controlled and progressive manner that doesn't send shock waves through the economy, markets and investors, we need to reduce the corporate and income tax rates at approx. 2% per year until they arrive at a 28% corporate flat tax and a 20% income flat tax that starts at income exceeding $24,000 annually. As we pay down our national debt, in the short term future, we should be able to realize a 25% corporate tax and an 18% income tax. Eventually, as we get a handle on our debt, we could enjoy a 22% corporate tax and a 15% income tax. These taxes would be flat across income brackets; however, there would be targeted tax credits that would stimulate the economy, job growth, and provide for charitable programs for those in need. Some of these targeted, economy-stimulating tax credit incentives include:

a) Dependent family members up to a max of 8 dependents per household

b) Business payroll expenses for domestic employees who are domestic residents

c) The purchase of and/or depreciation of equipment certified as being made in America or other approved countries with whom we have equitable fair trade

d) Charitable contributions

e) Interest on home loans for domestic residents

f) Interest on domestic loans for domestic business structures and domestic operations

g) Personal medical expenses beyond a predetermined threshold

h) Domestic commodity purchases as a business expense for domestic businesses

Other targeted tax credits could be added as they are found to have value and the potential to create positive stimulus for our country. Eligibility for these tax credits would be based on domestic interests and income tax brackets with those at the lowest tax bracket being eligible for additional tax credits than those at the highest tax brackets. Tax credits should serve a purpose in being a benefit to our country and society in some way. They should not be designed to benefit those who support foreign economies in the global market place. Why would we give tax incentives to those who export our jobs and domestic business interest abroad to other countries? Are we putting returns on investments ahead of our domestic economic health? Economically, we cannot afford a trade war with competing countries in the world marketplace--especially the ones who hold our debt and can raise the interest rate on that debt. Our debt has put us in the compromising position of having to clean up our own economic frugality and morality before we can rightly--and without arrogance--point out the frugality and morality of others. But just because we've compromised our position to levy import taxes doesn't mean that we can't target economic stimulus on our own soil, through targeted tax laws, that level the playing field with competitors in the global marketplace.

I suggest that domestic payroll expenses, paid to U.S. citizens in the United States, should be a targeted tax credit that benefits corporations who employ U.S. citizens in the United States. Those corporations who choose to conduct operations overseas should do so with no tax benefit for that expense from the U.S. The same principle should apply to domestic investments in facilities and real estate overseas. Investments overseas don't promote job growth and economic health domestically and should not be eligible as an expense for tax credit purposes. Any equipment bought by businesses and corporations in the U.S. that is not certified as being made in America or as being made by a nation who conducts fair trade with the U.S. should not be eligible to be claimed as a business expense for tax purposes. That means imported trucks, cars, heavy equipment, aircraft, boats, and all other types of equipment should not be eligible to be claimed for depreciation and as a business expense for tax purposes. We need to put Americans to work first and the rest of the world second, if they don't support fair market trade with the United States. Tax credits that give domestic incentives for investment in the American economy can be an effective tool in stimulating our economy and fair trade with our global economic competitors. We are the consumer capital of the world and we need to use that fact to our advantage. Our global competition might call into question import taxes on the global stage and market, but the right to target tax incentives for our citizens is a sovereign right and can be a very effective stimulus for our economy and jobs creation at home. We need to put America first. As other countries in the global marketplace align themselves in fair trade with the United States, then Congress could review and add their commodities as being eligible for tax credits to American businesses.

Should American prosperity return in the wake of these changes, a law should be passed that in addition to paying the annual interest on our debt, a minimum percentage of not less than 1% annually should be paid towards the principle of our debt and shall not be repealed until such time that we have no national debt.

18.Any government program that specifically taxes our society for a specific purpose should receive those taxes into an escrowed account. By a mandate of law, this money should not be used for any other purpose than the one for which those monies were obtained and entrusted to the government. To do so is a form of fraud and a misrepresentation of the purpose by which that money was received from society. A couple of government programs that fall into this category are social security and federal employees' retirement programs. For the government to take taxes from society under the pretense of a commitment, contract, and schedule of returning those funds to society and then defaulting on its original commitment, contract, and schedule is governmental fraud. Laws need to be passed preventing the misuse of taxes being placed in the general funds of the country when they were not obtained for that purpose. To do so is a clear misappropriation of government funds. If the government cannot honor its social security and retirement program commitments then those tax dollars were essentially back door increases in income taxes that went into the general fund for Congress to spend. If the government's definition of "misappropriation of funds" is the use of funds for anything other than that purpose for which those funds were specifically approved by law, then by the government's own definition, funds are misappropriated when used for purposes other than those for which those funds were obtained. The fact that they haven't created laws to prevent it is a matter of convenience and opportunity for them. That sounds like misrepresentation and fraud to me. What do **you** think?

19.There are a few injustices in our legal system that needs to be addressed. Any documentation required by the courts needs to be standardized and provided by the courts, so that the lay person can fill in the blanks with their personal information and pertinent details. That way, the lay person can represent themselves, if needed. The majority of Americans cannot afford the exorbitant prices charged for legal representation and our legal system isn't designed and supportive of someone representing themselves. This situation forces the majority of us to either go into debt that we can't afford or to lose by default. Justice for the American people isn't served by this situation, but governmental, mandated support of the legal profession is; it's a mandated subsidy through bureaucracy. For our government to require society to provide documentation in a format that requires more knowledge than what is freely provided through public education, then our government has placed conditions on justice being served based upon a person's working knowledge of our legal system. Really? We're more focused on proper documentation than justice being served. Forms and complete packets for each possible legal situation need to be provided by the government so that the legal standards and formats required by the courts can be maintained; but more importantly, justice and representation can be available to all classes of society. Society and justice deserve a system designed to be user-friendly and simple so that all levels of education and financial means in society will have the capacity to be represented in any court of law.

This next issue is more of a reality than an injustice, but one I have been made aware of through the plight of others (having never been a felon myself). While I believe in the punishment of those members of our society who have broken our laws, and that justice should be served, we need to consider the plight of those members of our society who have earned the title of "felon." After a person has earned the title of "felon," they cannot easily rent a place to live or find a place to work. With no place to live and no place to find work, how does this labeled citizen survive outside of criminal activity? We all have the right to know who that felon is, and we also have the right to not accept the risk of their presence should we not want to. For the felon, the prospect of returning to being a contributing, law-abiding member of society is a challenging one. The need for survival can tempt a person into criminal activity.

One potentially helpful remedy for this situation might be to allow employers to pay a lower minimum wage to felons for their first 6 months of employment probation, during which they have the opportunity to establish their character and reliability to their employer. Financial incentive for the employer, the burden of which would be carried by the felon through reduced wages, might stimulate both parties to overcome this situation. The felon should rightly carry this burden because they created the situation for themselves in the first place. What would be wrong is to put this burden on the taxpayer who didn't create the situation. Many times when our government is made aware of these situations in society, some misguided committee chairman in government will put the issues on the backs of the tax payers under the guise and guilt of obligation for the betterment of society. Many times, this kind of political philosophy couldn't be more wrong. Generally, it is far better to help people help themselves than to create government dependency at the expense of the tax payer, which creates greater dependency for all parties involved.

Another potential remedy for the survival of felons in our society is to use any social security benefits they might be entitled to underwrite and guarantee an initial one month's rent. This would give incentive and financial security to a potential landlord for giving a felon residence. The funds could only be received by a property owner who is listed as the felon's landlord, and who satisfies an established burden of proof and entitlement requirement. This residence incentive should only be available if the felon has paid into social security and has established funds there. A felon in our society is handicapped in their ability to survive and could be entitled to social security support through funds previously contributed by that felon.

The point is that if we give the felon the opportunity to survive in society, after having labeled them as such, their ability to return to being a contributing part of society is increased if we create a means of survival for them within the boundaries of the law.

20. "Pork barrel" politics is a plague that corrupts our government and needs to be stopped as soon as possible. Pork barrel politics is the currently accepted method of congressional representatives being allowed to add their own special interest perks and revisions to any legislation coming through Congress in return for their supporting vote. Basically, this is political blackmail and extortion. Congressional representatives are fundamentally saying, "If you buy off my vote, through what I want, I will support your bill; but if you don't, then I'm not supporting your bill."

This is corrupt and not the kind of compromise our Founding Fathers intended.

Any revision to any bill in Congress should have relevance to the same topic and purpose as the bill that was originally submitted, and should have some kind of supporting role in either limiting or expanding that bill. For example, if a bill's original topic and purpose is the building of an interstate overpass in Indiana, no one should be able to add a revision to that bill to fund a study for the mating habits of the spotted owl in Oregon. The two subjects are not related in any way and for them to be tied together in legislation doesn't make any sense; the coupling is based in coercion and is governmental corruption. We need to either limit revisions to bills, insisting they be relevant to the topic and purpose of the originally submitted bill or give the president the power of a line item veto to weed out this form of corruption. The power of a line item veto provides a major shift in power towards the presidential branch of our government and I don't believe our Founding Fathers would have supported it. The right thing would be for our congressional representatives to properly represent us and deliberate over the bills that come through Congress based on their merits of conscience, not their political opportunities --even if the integrity to properly represent us has to come through a system of limits and boundaries to guide them in their duties. Unfortunately, Congress has the conflict of interest in being the entity that establishes and sets the guidelines for itself. That's why I suggest the need for "local representatives" in Congress. Even if we found someone willing to submit such a bill--setting guidelines for the revision of bills in Congress-- Congress will resist giving up the power to add their own self-interest to bills that come before them. There are too many self-interested politicians who would vote against it.

This brings up a few fundamental problems. Our state representatives are there to rightfully get what they can for their state, but in issues that involve the good of our country as a whole, our government is lacking. The Senate was established to be a senior, stable influence that would (hopefully) deliberate from a position of increased integrity, experience, and national interest because of their longer terms In office. But when issues arise that involve changing or removing legislative power, there is a need for the people to be involved. "Local representatives" assigned to Congress is my proposed solution.

Another method could be a federal ballot initiative process through which the people could control their legislative branch of government-- especially when there is a conflict of interest situation that requires that branch of government to reduce its own power and limits or to regulate itself. After satisfying requirements proving the national popularity of an initiative, those initiatives could then be placed on the federal ballot during the election cycle to determine which initiative would go up for a vote during the following election cycle. If the ballot initiative doesn't pass, then it would again have to go through the qualifying and popular vote process. Allowing more than one federal ballot initiative at a time could cause chaos and instability in our government and is not recommended. This federal ballot Initiative would have to stand up to a constitutionality review by our judicial branch of government, as laws currently do. Also, instead of going through four years of bad legislation, the legislative branch of our government could repeal the federal ballot initiative if it is found by that body to be detrimental to our country.

In conclusion, "pork barrel" politics have been a problem in our country for quite some time, and it's obvious that we need to devise a way to pass those bills that have good merits while eliminating those revisions whose unrelated, special interest, and corrupt baggage clouds just exactly what is being voted for.

21.We need to simplify the immigration process to make it more practical and possible to effectively screen, document, and control immigrants entering this country. Our process is so burdensome and backlogged that our ineffective administration of processing immigrants contributes to people immigrating here illegally. As a country, we need to refocus our immigration policy towards protecting our society from criminals fleeing here from other countries, from diseases being carried in by immigrants, and from undocumented immigrants entering our country to financially drain our society.

No federal benefits should ever be extended to an undocumented immigrant who came here illegally. The only exception would be to render medical assistance to those with medical emergencies. States also should not extend benefits to illegal aliens and should be considered unsupportive of federal immigration policy if found doing so. This statehood status could limit federal funding of certain programs that could inadvertently benefit illegal aliens. Anyone found hiring illegal aliens should lose their business license for a time and should pay penalties. Anyone found to be in this country illegally should be deported after at least two weeks have passed, to allow for family members to contact each other. There are more effective means of securing our borders than we are currently deploying and this should be rectified. Every Illegal alien currently within our borders should be extended the opportunity to receive a green card or visa as appropriate. If all of the illegal aliens in our country were documented and contributing towards our prosperity, we would all be better off. Anyone found to be in violation of the terms of their immigrant status should be deported. English is and should always be our official language.

I have worked with many immigrants in my life and understand why they come here. I am sympathetic to their circumstances. We all need to contribute and benefit together as a society. We need to understand that immigrants are going to come to our country. If we promote their coming through the front door as a documented, contributing part of our society, instead of allowing illegal immigration through our back door, then we will all be better off. When we ignore and overlook illegal immigration, we lose not only the respect of those we're trying to deter from immigrating illegally but we lose the respect of our own society as well. With the proper laws, enforcement policy and organizational support, we can definitely do better than we are currently.

22.I would like to share a couple of opinions about the countries that collectively used to be called Russia during the cold war. It's true that Russia was once a communistic, political adversary with military influence, however, she has since turned away from the communist ideology and has been struggling to become a successful democracy for quite some time now-- long enough to show commitment, determination, sincerity, and willingness to sacrifice in pursuing a better way of life. Russia's citizens are hanging onto the dream of freedom, democracy, and prosperity that they predominately saw in us, the United States of America. It's true that we were Cold War adversaries, but we should remember that Russia was our ally in both World War I and World War II. Russians are a smart, capable people that have rivaled our own capacities in their abilities. They deserve our support, in the name of exporting democracy around the world, as much as any other nation we lend assistance to. My research tells me that the coalition of Russian countries have vast reserves of natural resources in oil, gas, minerals, mining products and timber--just to name a few. They have a huge potential for being a strong, free, democratic presence in northern Asia-- an anchor of economic stability and influence in the region. Russia could be the example and hope of freedom, rights, democracy and prosperity in that region that we have been for them. It is in our interest that they flourish as a democracy. I'm not aware of any religious, jihadist ambition of Russia's to annihilate the United States, and I would rather buy oil and goods from a committed, struggling democracy than from an avowed enemy.

The biggest reason the Middle East has the capacity to terrorize us and the rest of the world is because of the money they make from their oil reserves. That's where their military strength has come from-- not from their manufacturing capabilities or their natural resources, other than oil. It's obvious to me that as financial support of hostile Middle Eastern countries is decreased, so is their capability to export terrorism.

Wouldn't it be nice to have an international coalition of democratic oil producers to offset the influence that the Organization of the Petroleum Exporting Countries (OPEC) has on the price of oil and oil production globally? The democratic oil producers would be an alternative organization that disgruntled OPEC members and non-OPEC oil producers could look to for fair treatment, representation and coalition. The United States, The Russian coalition of countries, Iraq and others could be that alternative organization of oil-producing counties. We need to drastically reduce our dependence on oil--but until that time, wouldn't it be nice to know that there are nations in the world we can go to who exercise fair, free market practices to help stabilize the price and availability of oil products? Imagine the positive effects that would have on our economy.

CHAPTER FOUR

IF I WERE PRESIDENT

First, I'd like to point out that you can't legislate from the White House or from the presidential branch of our government. That's not the way our country is set up and rightly so--or else we would be a dictatorship. Congressional representatives are elected to represent their respective states. Supreme Court justices are the appointed representatives of our laws, our constitution, and our form of government. The president is the elected representative of the people and the nation as a whole. As a representative of the people, our president should be an outspoken representative and garner the support of those initiatives that are in the best interest of the nation. I can promise, without reservation, that if I were elected president, I would be a tireless, relentless, promoter of those things our nation stands in need of and that are in the best interest of our freedoms, our rights, our sovereignty, our safety, our constitution, and our form of government. If I were elected President of the United States, the priorities in my administration would be as follows:

1. **Reestablish Prosperity Economics:** As soon as possible, I would establish an economic policy that stabilizes our free market system, reestablishes health and confidence in our markets, and promotes a return to investment in our markets. This economic policy is to submit to congressional supporters initiatives that change our tax laws to a flat tax and tax credit incentive system of taxation. A willing

Congress should be able to implement these initiatives within 9 months. (See chapter 3, index 14 and 17 for more details.)

2. **Government Disclosure:** I would use those funds appropriate to be used by the president until such time as Congress could be convinced to provide federal support for the dissemination, in synopsis format, the voting record of the President of the United States, The Senate, The House of Representatives, and the decisions made by the United States Supreme Court annually. A local and accessible record of the activities of our federal representatives in our government should be maintained, for public review and scrutiny, in every post office in the country. Individual states should be welcome to maintain their records for public display at these locations as well. We are in dire need of transparency and accountability in our governments so that as informed voters, we can preserve our freedoms and retain control of our governments through accountability and involvement. (See chapter 3, index 7 for more details.)

3. **Restore Power Back to the People:** Through supportive members of Congress, I would advocate and promote legislation that shifts power in Washington D.C. back toward the states, and ultimately the people, by promoting a bill that effectively doubles the people's representation in the House of Representatives by adding "local representatives," as discussed earlier. This bill would also increase the representation in the Senate by the addition of "local senators," with every state governor becoming a satellite congressional member. I would also promote legislation that a state sponsored appointment to the U.S. Supreme Court

be filled by the collective vote of a quorum of state's attorneys general or an elected United States Attorney General. As with our legislative branch of government, our judicial branch stand's in need of shifting a little power back to the states. I also believe the people of our country have the right and deserve the power to more directly control their government and their own destinies through one federal ballot initiative every 4 year election cycle, and I would support legislation toward that end. (See chapter 3, index 1, 2, 3, 4, 5, 14 and 20 for more details.)

4. **Deter Corruption:** I would promote legislation prohibiting our politicians from practicing "pork barrel" politics. This legislation would require that revisions to any bill submitted to Congress must have some kind of supporting role in the same relevant topic and purpose for which the bill was submitted. (See chapter 3, index 20.)

5. **Deter Waste and Corruption:** Next, I would promote legislation requiring that any candidate for a government contract provide documentation and disclosure of all proposed materials and services in order to be eligible for consideration. This will dramatically reduce waste, corruption, and illegitimate proprietary leverage being imposed upon the government, while promoting healthy and fair competition among contractors. Thus, jobs will be created by the hundreds of thousands for our economy. (See chapter 3, index 12and 14.)

6. **The Fundamental Purpose of Patents is to Benefit Society:** Next, I would promote legislation that would simplify our patent laws to stimulate new business growth, investment and jobs. Another provision of this legislation would be to shorten potentially life-extending, medical patents and all pharmaceutical patents from 20 years to 10 years. New business ventures deserve the opportunity of a promising return on their investment, but extended returns at the expense of society's physical and financial health needs to be a compromised balance of returns to industry, versus the benefit to society, and therefore should be more limited in duration.

7. **Reduce Our Debt:** I would also promote a Budget Integrity Amendment that would not allow us to borrow more than 90% of our GDP unless we are in a state of national crisis declared by Congress. Also, any debt, previous or current, incurred by the United States shall be paid back annually at a rate that includes, after having paid the annual interest due on that debt, paying a minimum of 1% of the principal annually until it is gone. (See chapter 3, index 17 for more details.)

8. **Restore Government Integrity by Keeping its Promises to Society:** As the president, I would promote legislation requiring that any government program that taxes society for a specific purpose should receive those taxes into an escrowed account that, by law, cannot be used for any other purpose. (See chapter 3, index 18 for more details.)

9. **Restore Judicial Integrity and Representation through Simplicity:** I would promote legislation requiring the federal

and state governments to provide every juridical document required by the applicable courts in a "fill-in the-blanks" format, complete with block- by-block instructions for their use. Complete packets and/or a required documentation process list for every juridical process should enable citizens at every level of society to represent themselves in any civil and/or criminal court. The government should continue to provide needed legal representation for the accused in criminal courts. Government at all levels should still be able to determine and require the juridical documentation and processes that legislation supports, but all levels of society should be given the physical means of satisfying those demands and requirements, including those in society who do not have the financial means to hire legal expertise. Justice should not be tied to financial means, privileged knowledge, and/or elite requirements beyond what society's base level of understanding and financial means is. Justice should be available to all levels of society. Anything less is a progression from inclusive, public, justice, towards mandated, privileged treatment of a financially discriminate section of society. (See chapter 3, index 19 for more details.)

10. **Provide Governmental Support of Free Market Competition:** I would promote debate and potential legislation that would introduce government participation in our free market system. This will provide healthy competitive pressure and a stabilizing effect on our free market economy. Limited competition and/or pricing that respects competitor's profits reduces the available supply of goods and the buying power of society. The economy stagnates when profits are skimmed off the market by the privileged few, instead of those profits being reinvested in

the economy to the benefit of society. (See chapter 3, index 9 for more details.)

a. Pharmaceuticals are the first business segment I would promote government business participation in because they are linked to society's health and life span. Also, pharmaceuticals have artificially high prices with the capacity for large returns on investment. Government participation in this market could help reduce our national debt and/or tax requirement, and could be called into action to prevent epidemics or biological attacks. Competitive pricing in this business segment would also financially benefit society, including Medicare, Medicaid, and military health care costs.

b. Following successes with pharmaceuticals, I would promote government competition in the petroleum business segment. Our economic health, military costs and capabilities are dependent upon petroleum products and participation in this segment would benefit society, our military and our national defense. Because of our high demand for petroleum products, the additional supply availability could dampen price fluctuations, stabilize the economy, and provide another source of national debt reduction.

Other business segments could be evaluated and considered by our legislators as potential business ventures as society's needs dictate and the market's lack of competitive pressures indicate. These governmental business ventures that support and promote free market competition would have to be fair and equitable so as to not place an unfair burden on those business segments chosen for government participation. The goal should be to benefit our markets and our people so that society as a whole benefits from government participation. To put market concerns above the people's concerns or vice versa can be detrimental to both. Although I believe this to be generally unintentional, the bottom line effect is that currently we give priority to our markets in the hope that our society will benefit. I think we need to play a more active role in a way that doesn't diminish, stagnate, over regulate, or violate our free market system but involves us in a way that embraces and supports the genius of a free market society. Fair accounting, taxes and expenses would need to be calculated and assessed against these government business entities so that they compete fairly in the marketplace. All applicable corporate taxes, fees, and government-mandated expenses should be compared, averaged and assessed against these government entities and should be applied towards our national debt. The profits from these government business entities should be set high enough so as to not create an excess burden on those chosen business segments, but low enough that society will get an honest value at a reasonable price. A minimum profit margin of 25% and a maximum profit margin of 100% are recommended to our legislators. Our government could benefit from temporally higher profit margins during national crisis, such as the economic crisis we are in right now. Eventually, as our national debt becomes manageable, these controlled profits should help reduce our federal tax requirement.

11.**Include Our Military Experience in Our Military Decisions:** I would initiate debate and promote legislation that considers the role of the President of the United States being commander–in-chief, and if there might be a satisfactory method of including the experience of our career military commanders without relinquishing or jeopardizing control of our military by Congress and the people. (See chapter 3, index 15 for more details.)

12.**Constitutional Benefits from the Other Two Branches of Our Government:** I would promote legislation seeking to benefit from the experience gained by retired presidents and Supreme Court justices that have served us. Each retired president and Supreme Court justice should have the opportunity to submit one bill to Congress for deliberations by that body after their tenure, so that as a country we can benefit from the experience and knowledge they've gained while in our service. (See chapter 3, index 13 for more details.)

13.**Ensure Our Laws Regarding Government Corruption are Effective:** To eradicate nepotism from our government, I would promote legislation requiring genealogy information by all federal employees. I feel it's okay for government employees to be related, so long as those relations are not more concentrated than the local society at large, and those relations didn't play a role in those relatives obtaining employment. Currently, our laws regarding nepotism generally prohibit persons in supervisory positions from having relatives under their supervision or stewardship. As a government employee, I have seen organizational restructuring just to satisfy and keep relatives outside the legal definition of nepotism. The nepotism is still happening, but it's happening just outside the definition of the law so as to not be in violation of the law. Our laws aren't preventing nepotism; they are just requiring corrupt practices to be more creative at the expense of integrity and credibility in government. Issues like this give validation to the belief of corruption in our government and create despondency of society.

If we had genealogical information of government employees showing relationships, by blood and marriage, then those in charge of monitoring nepotism violations would have the information they need to effectively deter nepotism. Government employees should be hired and promoted based on their knowledge, skills, and abilities. They should not be discriminated against because of relations or any other discriminating factor, other than the government and tax payer getting the most qualified person for that position. Confidence and integrity needs to be restored to our government through practices that mandate fairness and prohibits discrimination through the excessive hiring of relatives and creating a corrupt government aristocracy. (See chapter 3, index 11 for more details.)

14.**Protect Our Public Lands for Access by All Levels of Society:** Our freedoms and this country were fought for so that every American might have the same right to enjoy and prosper in this great land. I would promote legislation that any state lands to be sold should first be offered to the federal government, giving the government the opportunity to secure those lands for the people and our country. Most of these lands were originally given by the government towards new state charters and it's reasonable to expect and require the states to give the government the first opportunity to reclaim those lands if they are no longer desired by the states. The American people deserve the opportunity to enjoy and experience these lands for themselves and their posterity. Their tax dollars are given in support of their country and their state and it is reasonable to expect that the elected stewards of their public land resources should not take away their access to these lands through mismanagement and/or their sale to private entities. It should take voter approval to sell state and national lands, not the approval of a misguided elected official. Many lands are regularly being bought by private entities that, in turn, restrict access to these once public natural resources--unless you can afford the fees they impose. Their use is limited to those who have the financial means to pay for access to enjoy these lands. It is not in our interest to sell our country to private or foreign investors. I believe it is in the interest of the common citizens of our country, the public, to preserve the condition of and the opportunity for access to these natural resources. All classes of society pay taxes towards their stewardship and all classes deserve representation and access to these resources. Access to our national resources should not be based on our class position in society.

15. **Outlaw the Potential and Temptation for Corruption in Government:** I would promote legislation that would make it illegal for any elected or appointed government official or their staff, who receives wages and/or compensation from taxpayers to accept any form of compensation from any other entity during their tenure. This should apply to all three branches of government. I believe citizens should have a right to group together around common goals and interests and to lobby their government officials in support of those interests. I believe it prudent to require those who lobby government officials to register, so as to declare their existence, their intentions and to make known those things to the public. It should be illegal, however, to lobby elected or appointed government officials or their staff through unregistered channels that are hidden from public view and scrutiny. If these disclosure requirements are already in place, so much the better. But for elected or appointed

government officials or staff to receive any form of compensation from those other than those by whom they were elected or appointed to represent creates an inherent conflict of interest and should be against the law. Laws should exist to establish boundaries of conduct that deter misrepresentation or illegal activities and to promote actions of integrity and virtue.

For example, if a lobbyist organization wants a sympathetic and supportive government official or staff member to be a keynote speaker at a function, then that official or staff member should be motivated to do so by his or her convictions of conscience, not by compensations of monetary value. Their compensation should be the privilege of supporting something they believe in and should not be swayed by ulterior, financial motives. Elected or appointed government officials and staff are being paid for their service and have already received a just compensation from the taxpayers they represent. To receive compensation from any other source opens the door for corruption in government and creates the conflict of interest in being compensated by more than one source. To accept the election or appointment of being a government official or staff member is to accept being in the service of the represented taxpayers. It is a position of service whose focus should be on the people served, and not on the compensation. Any politician who wants to receive compensation in the private sector should leave government service and work in the private sector. Serving the people as an elected or appointed representative is a calling of service and conscience, not self-serving personal ambitions. It shouldn't be about the money or compensation. Our Founding Fathers argued against compensation for government officials precisely for the potential of corruption we have witnessed in some of our government officials. If government officials are to be compensated, then laws should be passed protecting society from the potential for their corruption.

Is it a conflict of interest to have government officials hearing from a lobbyist from whom they've received compensation? Of course it is! If a lawyer is hired to represent a certain party, and if he accepts compensation from and provides part- time representation for the opposing party, is he found to have a conflict of interest? Of course he is, and is deterred from doing so by laws prohibiting the practice. When we as a society trust the character and integrity of our officials over the boundaries and guidelines they morally need, then as a society we put ourselves at risk for corruption and deserve the corruption we get for having put our head in the sand. If we can safely trust and believe in the integrity of humankind, then why do we have laws? Why not just trust everybody to be good? Because the weakness and depravity of men and women has proven that we can't be trusted--that even good men and women need boundaries to teach them the path of integrity and virtue. Every path, even those in life, has a boundary on both sides! We shouldn't trust and/or tempt elected or appointed government officials or staff by allowing them to be pulled in conflicting directions through conflicting compensations and loyalties. Our laws should set boundaries to prevent it and a means to prosecute it when it happens.

16.**Use our World Status as a Consumer Nation to Our Advantage:** I would promote economic and political diplomacy that recognizes nations and governments with a favorable trade status--those who practice fair, considerate, respectful, and non-aggressive economic, environmental, military, and diplomatic policies towards the U.S. and the world community of nations. And for those nations and governments who choose to practice unfair, inconsiderate, and aggressive economic, environmental, military, and diplomatic policies and behavior would receive a recognized unfavorable trade status and would be excluded from any form of economic trade with the U.S. This unfavorable trade status would extend to those nations who choose to continue trade with these rogue elements. As a nation or government, if you want to enjoy a favorable trade status with one of the largest consumer nations on the planet then you must play fair and recognize our need for fair play from others, or you lose this valuable economic opportunity and status.

17.Integrity and the Presidential Administration of Our Government: My first priority would be to promote the solutions to those issues and concerns outlined in this book. I feel they need to be put before the American people to be discussed, debated and implemented, as there is sustaining support by the people. If I were President of the United States, I would maintain an unwavering focus on the reality that I am a representative of the people and our country first and of the rest of the world second.

The president, or his designated representative, should attend all crises, events or priorities that have the collective concern of our nation as a whole. The American people deserve to have on the ground, wherever needed, their elected representative personally overseeing the collective concerns of our country. As commander-in-chief, any national holiday that honors the service of our military, past and present, demands the presence and representation of that position at a level and authority that gives honor and reverence to those who have earned that respect. I would never compromise the position or the freedoms of the United States to any ally, nation, world organization or entity.

I would rally the American people to get involved in their government and those solutions we stand in need of. I would publicly promote and advertise impending decisions coming up for vote on Capitol Hill so that whatever your position is, as an American, you will be informed and have the opportunity to get involved through your congressional representatives. Then, as a follow up, I would make available the results of these votes, along with how each representative voted, so that as Americans and voters you will be informed as to how you are being represented. Then, as informed voters, you will be prepared for the next election. I would establish this precedence of informing the American public so that it might hopefully continue in the future.

I would address all the issues that come before the nation and presidency with all the solemnity, thoughtfulness, research, consultation, and prayer that those decisions having national consequences, obligations, and commitments deserve. I would use all of those political, diplomatic, economic, military, intellectual, and national resources available to the United States to the benefit and preservation of our freedoms, our form of government and our country.

CHAPTER FIVE

PERSONAL HISTORY

My name is Jeffrey Clinton Bradford. I was born in Cumberland County, Fayetteville, North Carolina on September 24th 1963. Fayetteville is close to Fort Bragg, North Carolina. My father was stationed with the U.S. Army 82nd Airborne Division there at the time I was born. I grew up as a military dependent that lived in many different places, and I was exposed to many different cultures and ethnic backgrounds during this time. The places I've lived that stick out the most in my mind are Stuttgart, Germany; Fort Lewis, Washington; Fort Rucker, Alabama; and Santaquin, Utah, where my father retired after 20 years of military service.

My school experiences ranged from being a minority in school while attending large intercity schools to the small rural school experience. My parents, for the most part, found housing accommodations in rural communities, which were close to where we were stationed. My childhood experiences were influenced by living in those regions of our country instead of living on military bases. The experiences of my childhood, the example of my parents, and my associations in life have left me with a love, appreciation, and many friendships with many races and classes of people. I can safely say, without reservation, that I don't have a prejudiced bone in my body. I grew up repeatedly being the "new kid on the block" amongst people who were lifelong friends. This environment caused my personality to be humble, friendly, and respectful--all of which was reinforced by my military-oriented parents. I enjoyed participating in rodeos as a youngster and was an avid bull rider, bareback rider, and roper in my youth.

I began employment and hard work at the early age of 14 as a ranch hand in the state of Washington and have been working hard ever since. In school, I was a very capable student that knowledge and understanding came to me easily. This facilitated my ability to work, due to not having to study too hard to test well. During my school years I worked as a ranch hand, a laborer, a roofer, a forklift operator, an industrial equipment operator, a production assembler and a dishwasher.

After graduating from high school I obtained employment as an apprenticing helicopter mechanic. During this time of apprenticeship, I started dating my first wife and we were married. She had a beautiful, six month-old daughter named Britany, whom I adopted at the age of 4. My first son, Austin, was born in March of 1985 while I was in basic training for the U.S. Army. Both of my children are a source of love, pride and happiness. Near the end of my apprenticeship in helicopter maintenance, I decided to join the U.S. Army as a Blackhawk Helicopter mechanic with the goal of going to flight school to become a helicopter pilot during my enlistment. I went to night school while in the military to obtain my FAA-certified, Airframe and Power Plant, aircraft mechanic's license. After 11 credit hours of college, I realized that I was just paying the teacher to give me reading assignments that I understood and then asking me if I had any questions. Well, I understood what I read and I didn't have any questions so I opted out of the program. I reread the entire course material one more time and passed the three required written tests, one each for generals (math, geometry, electrical, etc), one each for airframes and one each for power plants. Then I took the oral and practical test, which tested my knowledge of airframe and power plant systems on an actual aircraft. I scored a 98% on my generals, a 100% on my airframe, and 100% on my power plant tests to get my FAA Airframe and Power Plant license that should have taken me two years in college.

During my last year in the military, I applied for flight school. Unfortunately, my application came back near the end of my enlistment with a setback; my blood pressure was too low during post-exercise testing. I had physically trained hard for over a year to be ready and was in pretty good shape, and after a week-long evaluation with my blood pressure being good, my packet was resubmitted. I applied for an extension of my separation date in the hopes that my application would go before the flight school selection board. Another setback came in the form of the Gramm, Rudman, and Hollings Bill, which required the military to shorten the separation dates in an effort to save money. This act in Congress overrode the authority of my previously approved extension and forced me out of the military before I could get a response back from the Warrant Board. I separated from the military only to find out weeks later that although funding cuts had reduced the number of available flight school positions in half, I had still made the cut and was accepted into flight school--but this was invalid because of my separation status. My desire to become a helicopter pilot didn't come to fruition.

Just before my separation from the military, my second son, Weston, was born. He is also a source of joy, pride, and happiness in my life. After my military service, I temporarily worked as a production welder while waiting to regain employment with the helicopter company I had worked for previously. I might mention that many of these employment opportunities had skill tests associated with them. The first time I ever MIG welded was the day I tested for the production welder job, and I passed well enough to get the job. I told them I had welded before, but my experience was arc welding in high school and they gave me a shot anyway. After my return to working on helicopters, this time as a licensed journeyman mechanic, I settled into working in a hangar environment, honing my skills and expertise.

Eventually, as I was prepared and found opportunity, I began working as a field mechanic to increase my pay enough to move our little family from our two-bedroom apartment into a modest three-bedroom home. As a field mechanic, I worked on a rotating schedule--predominantly in Alaska, but eventually many places from the Canadian and Mexican borders to the Rocky Mountains and West Coast. The company I was working for filed for bankruptcy in 1993, and this started a trail of having worked for many different employers in an effort to support my family. Although I love working on helicopters, a couple of times I left aviation employment from frustration over its instability as a means of employment. During my time as a helicopter mechanic, I also worked as a truck driver pulling "doubles;" a high-speed, manufacturing equipment mechanic; a heavy equipment and semi truck mechanic; and a millwright at a steel mill. Through all of this movement in employment, I always left on terms of being rehired. Throughout that time, I only drew three unemployment checks and every time I saw how small it was I knew I had to get employment quickly. Fortunately, I was blessed to find work when I needed it. Some of this employment movement was due to employer bankruptcy, some of it was seasonal work, and some were progressions onto better employment.

This timeframe was also a period of spiritual growth for me and I began to have a yearning to know more about the scriptures and Jesus Christ. In 1998, after a couple of years of personal investigation, I realized that my scriptural knowledge was growing but my personal relationship with Jesus Christ wasn't. I could see the people around me expressing a personal relationship with Christ that I didn't feel I had. In seeking the answers why, I searched the Bible and my soul—which made me realize that I stood in need of repentance. After a couple of weeks of research and anxiety on how best to proceed, I came to the conclusion that I must do as the Bible directs; that is, confess my sins, make restitution wherever I could, forsake my sins to commit them no more, and follow the teachings of Christ. After having confessed my sins as required by an honest repentance I climbed the highest mountain peak above our home, about a 5000 foot climb, and knelt in prayer for a long time. After having prayed over everything in my heart I laid down to rest to ponder my life and what my future had in store. On that day, I felt the Lord's presence and obtained the relationship and testimony I was seeking with Christ.

I also learned a hard lesson when I got home; the Lord has an infinite capacity for understanding and forgiveness, but human beings do not. My wife had harbored a disposition towards ending our relationship for most of our marriage and this repentance process was just the excuse she was looking for. My wife and I had struggled to find happiness throughout our relationship. She was not comfortable with being affectionate, especially in public, and had recently told me in regards to my wanting our relationship to be emotionally closer that I was asking for something she couldn't give me. We had talked about her first marriage of six months for most of our 14-year marriage. She finally moved back in with her first husband for a brief time shortly after her relationship with her third husband failed.

These bitter lessons were not borne in vain, as I learned valuable things from the experience. I learned about the qualities a person would need and what type of person I might look for in any future attempts at love. These trials of my character and faith were very difficult, but they strengthened me and helped me to become the person I am today. The relationship I had gained with Christ came at the high price of some worldly consequences but the peace and knowledge of Christ's presence in my life has sustained and blessed me ever since. About seven months after my divorce was final, and the necessary healing had taken place in my heart, I began to date. I met my best friend, companion, soul mate, lover, and the love of my life on the 20th of February 1999. She still blesses my life today with all of those meaningful qualities and sources of happiness that blessed me then. After an unforgettable courtship, we were married on July 23, 1999. This marriage blessed my life with three more children, whose names are Jamie, Brittany, and Cody, whom I love as my own. My wife and I are also blessed with good relationships with the spouses of our children and our beautiful grandchildren, of whom we have seven to date.

In February 1999, I obtained employment as a contractor for the United States Air Force, then as a civil service employee overhauling flight control components. I have been serving my country as a civil service employee ever since. During this time of employment, I progressed from being a journeyman mechanic to a work leader who trained and led others in their duties. I then attended an 18-month course, sponsored by the Air Force, in leadership development training. This course was a blended course of on-base and off- base college classes with an emphasis on English, communication skills, lean manufacturing techniques, and successful psychological habits. I applied myself to the best of my ability in this endeavor and obtained a 4.0 grade point average and made the Weber State University Honor Society while I was attending there. After this, I performed the duties of a production supervisor over a production crew as a temporary detail for five months. During this time, our crew reached its production goal for on-time delivery, which wasn't happening before my tenure and hasn't happened since. Unfortunately, politics played a bigger role in the permanent selection of supervisor than my shop's productivity successes and my supervisory experience. My successor took over with little mechanical experience and no supervisory experience but was very successful in his ability to network with those who were in charge of the selection process. I returned to my position as a work leader with a renewed appreciation of helping others and being successful in my ability to overcome the challenges our shop routinely faced. More recently, I accepted a position as an = industrial engineering technician who plans the work, labor, and material needs for a shop similar to the one I used to work in.

That's a very short summary of my life to date. There are many other untold experiences throughout my life that aren't described. One such experience was building an apparatus that I invented and developed over a ten-year period. I applied for and obtained a patent and sold this apparatus to a reputable company on the East Coast.

Another experience that produces a statement I want to share is as follows: I once worked for a helicopter company that was going through some lean financial times. Field support was just barely enough—and sometimes lacking altogether. The lead mechanic on our maintenance crew came up to me and said, "Bradford, you and I are going to the front office to talk to the CEO of this place and straighten out our support problems." He was obviously upset. I said, "Okay, let's go." After a brief conversation with the CEO's secretary, we entered his office. My lead mechanic didn't even say hello; he immediately started into a laundry list of complaints. The CEO patiently waited and when my lead mechanic finished, the CEO asked him a question. He said, "What is your solution to this problem? How can we resolve this?" My lead mechanic replied, "I don't know. That's your job to figure out. I'm the one that needs these things fixed." Then the CEO said something I shall never forget. He looked the lead mechanic straight in the eye and said, "If you're not part of the solution then you are part of the problem!" I don't know if he had heard that statement somewhere before, or if he made it up in the heat of the moment, but I remember thinking to myself, "Now those are some profound words to live by right there." After the lead mechanic ended up on the receiving end of the conversation, he didn't know what else to say and we left. He didn't make the effort to research or devise solutions to his problems--he just threw a tantrum about what his complaints were, which didn't serve any constructive purpose. America, if we don't get involved and become part of the solutions for our country, then we are part of the problem. Our government, freedoms, and rights need our oversight, our solutions, and our involvement.

In review I have many military, government, civilian, educational, and life experiences, all of which have prepared me with the knowledge, perspective and common sense to navigate me through the challenges of life. These qualities, principles and attributes I have developed through the experiences of my life I offer and pledge as a source of ingenuity, value and service to those within my circle of influence.

CHAPTER SIX

SOME PARTING THOUGHTS TO CONSIDER

Thomas Jefferson, after thorough and extensive research on the known governments of the world, stated that the Anglo-Saxon people had created the greatest government ever devised by the wit of man. The Anglo-Saxon people, believed to be the "lost ten tribes of Israel" who traveled to the north, had a government that was patterned after the ancient nation of Israel. This ancient form of representative government was followed and patterned after by our Founding Fathers because it had the greatest longevity and success of the known representative governments in world history. The bottom line is that this inspired form of government came from God through revelation to Moses and his father-in-law, Jethro. Our government today falls short of that level of representation and, as James Madison stated, in reference to the golden age of the democracy in Athens, history has shown that more representation isn't always better. They fully debated and implemented the best they could within the boundaries of what society could bear at the time. Do we believe our constitution is perfect and above revision? Our Founding Fathers didn't. That's why they made provision to correct their mistakes, their oversights, and any unforeseen changes and requirements there might be in the future.

We started out with a two political party test of wills almost from the beginning and we've been cycling back and forth through voter frustration and uprising, trying to fix things ever since. A key reason why we were able to obtain the level of compromise and quality legislation that produced our constitution was because at the time of the Constitutional Convention, we had 13 different political parties. The compromise, focus, consideration, and worthwhile legislation that can come from a diversity of political power and opinion should not be underestimated and should be created today to foster the best legislation that can be obtained. Granted, the character of the delegates was an important component, but the diversity of motivations created a structure and recipe for compromise that eventually benefitted all parties. When that is achieved, so is true freedom through effective representation. All of that being said, the only way I can think of today to prevent the proven, inevitable contest and stalemate of our government, due to having only two viable political parties, is to create a greater division with more check and balance between federal, state and political party representation. This will foster compromise and national priority, instead of political advantage and ambition. Granted, the two political parties will still be present in both the federal and state entities, but the arrangement restores power back unto the states and creates more diversity due to different motivations between the states, the federal government, and the political parties. Also, different regional priorities will create diversity and better representation.

The added representation in Congress through the local representatives and governors I propose, will introduce representation from leaders who are actually governing and legislating in their home states. Instead of two political parties these allegiances will be further dispersed into state, federal, our political parties and the executive branch. We will have a similar political structure and representation that produced our constitution. We will have a similar recipe and formula for compromise and state-driven legislation that our Founding Fathers had. We should always be united as a nation on national priorities, but our representation should recognize our local concerns as well. Drawing power back toward the states and the people effectively does that and is in line with where our Founding Fathers felt our governmental power should originate and be. Our Founding Fathers also had reservations about too much judicial power; I believe judicial power should be drawn back down toward the states and people as well. That is where Supreme Court judicial opinion is implemented, and because of this, representation should be included from there.

A very important key representation element is in creating congressional, local representatives in government. To be eligible to serve as a local representative, as selected by and from the available Congress persons in your respective state's legislature, you or your voting district cannot have served in that capacity more times than other districts or your congressional peers. This is a huge improvement in effective representation for society and ensures that every voting district, in every state in the country, is eventually represented in federal government. The majority and the minority could both be represented. The majority would still be structured to rule, but a provision for the minority to be heard and represented would be created. This local representation includes those states that elect "at large" instead of voting districts, because every member in the state legislature will eventually have a turn at being a local representative, thereby providing representation for those who voted for that Congress person. The possibility that every American could really be represented in federal government is one that I know our Founding Fathers would have approved of, and so deserves our careful consideration. The combination of seated members and local representatives in government provides for representation of the majority and the minority in society. This arrangement could be further tiered down in state government to provide satellite representatives from progressively more local governments from state through county down to representation being originated from city governments, if states so desired. A representative government, similar to that of the Anglo-Saxon government that Thomas Jefferson dreamed of, could be realized with the right minor changes, vision, and implementation.

Our country was in its infancy when our Founding Fathers created our constitution within the boundaries of what society could accept and bear at the time. We have progressed into a mature nation with full commitment and participation in our union of states, and although most of the principles in our constitution are timeless in their value, some areas could benefit by some extremely careful refinement. The inherent stalemate of a two-party system was almost immediately obvious to our Founding Fathers after our government was formed. I believe that many good, brilliant, and capable minds have represented us in government and have, at one time or another, suggested what we stood in need of as a country and its issues. But the quagmire, corruption and ineffective stalemate created by a two-party system is holding us back from improving our lives and our situation. Our political responses don't satisfy our needs--they satisfy special interest and political ambitions instead of what's collectively good for our country. We stand in need of very careful and thoughtful change, with the hopes of those changes being implemented instead of becoming governmental stalemate victims.

In review, some fundamental problems I feel we have are as follows:

- Our government structure entitles Congress to regulate itself.
- We don't have state, segregated, independent influence and oversight over Congress.
- We don't have state, independent influence and oversight over the Supreme Court.
- Our commander–in– chief is not required to consider military knowledge and experience.
- Our country is being purchased at an alarming rate by private entities. Our public lands are fast becoming private access only.
- We need to be provided with credible, unbiased information about our government and its operation so we can be informed voters in order to better protect our interests, rights, freedoms and way of life.

We have a potential "Achilles heel" in our government because Congress is left to regulate and control itself. Our only recourse with bad representation in Congress is to vote, which is done in hindsight after the damage has already been done. Obama Care is a prime example, and there are many others in history that have come through both parties. We have to live with Congress' mistakes until they can be repealed and those who voted in the bad legislation can be voted out. A lot of damage can happen to our country until that takes place.

Congress is in the position of setting their own schedule, pay rate, and rules by which they operate. There's a wide open door for corruption and excesses in government. The only thing stopping them from becoming entrenched in privileged corruption is their own integrity and our oversight, as was admonished by our Founding Fathers. Our Founding Fathers read about, knew and understood the depravity of man and its existence is proven by history and some of our own politicians. History says that the integrity of our congressional representatives is going to be uncommon, and that leaves us with one barrier in preventing our government from becoming corrupt, excessive, an increasing burden and from infringing upon our rights. Currently, we are the one barrier! Our vigilant oversight and control is the one barrier that our Founding Fathers repeatedly admonished us about. How has your vigilant oversight and research of congressional initiatives been going lately? I don't know about you, but I find my own a little lacking. I'm trying to be involved and understand what's going on but I feel like my knowledge of what's really going on in our behalf is colored by where you get your information from. We can choose from a biased political party or a biased media. Either way, we're not sure what's really going on or what's been done until after the fact, when we hear about it in the hopefully unbiased news. That's why I'm saying as a country we need to devise an effective way for our states to oversee and influence the decisions made in Congress.

I wish Madison would have devised the government structure necessary for the states to oversee and influence our Congress--that guy was the master when it came to devising governmental structure to fulfill a purpose or satisfy a need. I believe this was an oversight that wasn't so obvious during their time because they intervened to establish proper government. Why would they believe that their posterity wouldn't do the same? They set the example and didn't have any reason to believe it wouldn't be followed. They had fairly open access to the government of their time. The biggest challenge they had in getting access to their government was transportation. I don't know about you, but I'm tired of getting form letters from senators thanking me for my interest in government. I want to talk to somebody that will do something for me. In our day, we have endless bureaucracy and red tape to wade through to try to influence our government.

I believe we need local representation. We need someone with a vote who can make a difference. We need someone with a state perspective instead of just a national or federal one. The constitutional convention option of influencing our government has never been done because of its risk to do more harm than good. So are we just stuck with what we have, really? We're just going to roll over and suffer with the lament that there's nothing that can be done? That's not what our Founding Fathers would have done. When they were faced with a situation they didn't like or that they disagreed with they did something about it. They researched what the best answers were and then they pursued the success of what they believed to be right with unwavering commitment. Our Founding Fathers left us with the task of overseeing and controlling our government for our society to survive and to prevent corruption from overrunning our government. Folks, we are not getting it done. Our vote isn't making enough of a difference--and then that vote is in hindsight after the damage has already been done. Corruption is slowly overtaking us, one bad congressional bill at a time. We need posted, assigned, vigilant guards and sentinels, at the state level, to oversee our future, our rights, and our prosperity. If there is anyone out there with more effective ideas about how to provide this oversight, without violating the rights of freedom, our country is in need of your insights.

My answer is local representatives and governors that are living in and are surrounded by the concerns of their home state to help them keep focus and perspective as they represent our interest in congressional decisions. As a member of state legislature, or as the governor of our state, they will be more aware of the impact that federal congressional bills will have on their home states. They will have state background information that our current representatives and senators are not even aware of to help them make their decisions. Local representatives and governors being segregated from Congress will be somewhat insulated from the concentration, influence and corruption of party politics in Washington D.C. They will be more accessible to the people because they will be among us.

I should point out that I don't believe it's in our best interest for state government to be more influential than the federal government. We already tried that under the Articles of Confederation and it didn't work. We will always need national vision, protection, regulation, collective strength and perspective that come from our presidential, congressional, and Supreme Court branches of our government. I believe those branches should be segregated from the states in a federal, national setting as they are, in order to gain and represent a national focus and vision for our country. For our federal government to be effective, it needs to have greater oversight and influence over the states. But the states need to have enough oversight and influence over the federal government to ensure the states' interests are represented and their rights are protected. I believe we need to increase the state-backed influence in our government. We are experiencing the effects of the concentration of power in Washington D.C. that Thomas Jefferson warned us about, and we need to pull back a little representative power toward the states so that we can effectively protect our rights and represent our interests in our government.

Religion is such an important issue in the lives of so many of us that I feel it necessary to discuss it as it relates to our country and government. First, let me say that our Founding Fathers wisely understood that religious persecution and the pursuit of religious freedom were some of the major driving forces behind immigration to America. They also understood that religion has as much potential to tear our nation apart as it does to bind us together. They wisely chose to insist on the separation of church and state to prevent the inevitable contest and comparison of different religious sects and beliefs, and to protect religious freedoms. Our Founding Fathers, as men of strong religious beliefs and convictions, chose to honor religious freedom more than their own personal religious preferences. This is a testament and an acknowledgment by them that freedom is an eternal principle supported by religious beliefs.

Commitment to religion is a personal choice and relationship that can't be sponsored or mandated by government, a political vote, or anyone else without violating religious freedom.

The Founding Fathers established freedom of religion in such a way that not only respected an individual's rights to worship as a matter of conscience, but they chose to recognize those aspects that were common to our religious beliefs in order to unite and bind us together. For example, our early government included the words "In God We Trust" on all of our money. In so doing, they reminded us of a common belief in Deity that respected all of our religions. Another testament of our Founding Fathers' religious beliefs is the fact that the Bible's book of Deuteronomy was referenced in patterning some of the structure and principles written into our constitution and form of government. The facts of our government's creation clearly indicate that one of the main purposes for the separation between church and state was to protect religious freedom, which includes the right of religious expression. Separation between church and state was never meant to be misconstrued as justification for abolishing religious expression by or from our representative form of government. Our Founding Fathers established many physical, intellectual, internal, and external religious representations of the will of the people throughout our government. The Constitutional Convention, at one point, was at an impasse--until Benjamin Franklin called for the opening of each day's session with a word of prayer in gratitude for their blessings and in supplication for inspiration toward their endeavors. It's obvious by the history and actions of our Founding Fathers that they felt that a person has as much right to pray in public and exercise free religious expression as it is the right of citizens to not display a belief in religion. Early American schools studied from the Bible, and prayer in school was an acceptable expression of religious freedom that was commonly practiced.

A fundamental structure and provision of our form of government is to adhere to the will of the majority in society while protecting the rights of the individual. If the majority of our society has faith in Deity, then prayer to that Deity in school or any other public or private place should be a matter of free religious expression, and this right should never be sequestered, barred, or restricted by government. To do so violates freedom of religion and expression.

The recognition and paying tribute to the existence of Deity through the creation, maintenance, and support of artifacts, edifices, monuments, buildings, libraries, museums, or any other structure supported by the majority, is a representative display of the will of our society. Thus, our government has every right and responsibility to do so. For our government to do anything less than to represent the will of the majority diminishes the representative claim and nature of our government. Our Founding Fathers established this practice because their vision was one of creating a representative government by its external representation, as well as its internal structure and operation.

For those of you in this country who are atheist, our freedoms provide you every right to your beliefs. But until your beliefs represent the majority in this country, you are not entitled to a government that eliminates representative expression of the will of the majority just to satisfy your minority viewpoint. To do so violates the very nature and claim of our government being a representative institution. The Ten Commandments from the Holy Bible is a religious goal, commitment, and belief that is common to the early American religious beliefs that this country was founded upon. As such, it is completely appropriate that the Ten Commandments be displayed on any structure chosen by the majority in our society. Public and private prayer is acceptable anywhere in America, and any deterrence of it is a violation of religious freedom.

Inspiration has played a huge role in the writing of this book. Because of this, I have felt obligated to write something promoting the restoration of religious freedom and expression in our country out of respect and appreciation for that Deity that is the source of my inspiration. The things I have written in this book, for the most part, came by inspiration—although I have done some reading and research.

I have generally been a mechanic of some kind for most my life. I've always wanted to attend college, but have always put the need to provide for my family above my own aspirations. I've always admired those who've been able to go to college. As a family, we could have sacrificed, I guess, while I went to school--but that never felt right to me and I couldn't see how we could ever afford it. I have always lived from paycheck to paycheck, working a full-time job with overtime, and the time or money for school never seemed realistic to me.

I'm not sure why, but lately I've been driven to learn more about our country's revolutionary beginnings. I recently read a series of books about our early history and it was one of the biggest reading endeavors I've ever accomplished--about 5,000 pages over nine books. Then, just as I finished this foundation of learning, there sprang up in our neighborhood an informal, college-level class on American history called "Foundations of Liberty." This class included a heavy reading assignment with a four-hour discussion and teaching lesson that followed about every six weeks. After about a year of having digested these nuggets of American history, I found myself being inspired with political thoughts and realizations about what I had been reading. As a mechanic, I have a predisposition for looking at things against the grain and outside of the box, trying ways of fixing and improving those things around me. So instead of forgetting these thoughts and ideas, I decided to write them down as they came to me. The more I wrote them down, the more my mind was inspired with deeper thoughts about the things I was realizing and considering. At first I wrote them down, and then later I decided to compile them into the book you are reading now. The value of the things I have written will only be realized if they are discussed, debated, found worthy of public support, and implemented to the benefit of our country.

My initial thoughts on implementation were to share these thoughts with those in government who have the influence and position to promote these ideas. Then I realized that they have been part of the problem. Without the vision with which these thoughts and solutions were formulated, those persons would be like a foreigner in a strange land. These ideas would just be unfamiliar words without the passion and vision that created them. Some people in government have arrived there by less than virtuous means, and finding those who have virtue in our government is like trying to find a needle in a haystack. I considered doing this myself, but apparently federal law doesn't allow federal employees to run for political office and it limits their involvement in partisan politics. (Political Activities Flyer - December 2011/ Hatch Act (5 USC 7321-7327) and regulations (5 CFR Part 734 B and C) I don't remember reading that in the fine print when I was hired. My question is this: how do incumbent, political, federal employees get around not violating this law unless this is another one of those special exclusions that doesn't apply to them? Anyway, I don't have the financial means to be unemployed and run for political office so my circumstances exclude me from running.

The best answer for implementation is **you** and your involvement. Without **you,** it doesn't matter what anybody thinks because **you** are the driving force required to make real change happen. Without **you,** these ideas will just be another set of political ideas that were offered at a moment in time when society didn't have the desire or care to entertain them. **You** are in the driver's seat and if **you** feel like you're not, then we need to stand up and **take America back** until we once again feel like we are in the driver's seat. Which presidential candidate do **you** feel can implement those things that **you** feel we stand in need of? Choose based on conscience and your beliefs--not party, ethnicity, or gender.

Time spent in political service for me does not qualify someone to be President of the United States. I'm looking for someone who has experienced the problems we face so there is a level of true understanding by that candidate. The role of governor, for me, is a good proving ground in preparation to be president. Please dig into this presidential election and be an informed voter. Right now, we need some serious help by the right person with integrity, virtue, business savvy, ingenuity and vision.

Don't let your future be decided by someone else's vote. I believe that if you don't vote, you don't have a right to complain.

I want to especially see solutions for those problems that jeopardize our ability to prosper and endure into the future in freedom. Consider some of the changes I'm talking about. These are not sterile little changes that can give someone the title of being different or promoting change without taking the risk of challenging the status quo. They are changes that challenge and withdraw power from the status quo. The one hope of support I have, in a lot of what I'm proposing, is from understanding, sympathetic people like **you**. I'm hoping that every state legislature and citizen will take a serious look at what I propose and support representative power being shifted back towards them and the people.

As a society, we are capable of being involved in our government and making sound decisions. Our early American citizen forbearers were not privileged to have the access and ease of information and education about what is needed in our government like we are. We live in the information age where the only thing holding us back in our ability to understand what is needed in government is our desire to apply ourselves and find out. The technology is available to make it easy for us to at least be informed voters so that we can protect our freedoms and our interests. The fact that the government isn't providing this information for local review, because we either don't demand it or they don't really want our involvement, is a shame on both our parts. Both sides need to get off their backsides and start doing the right thing before it's too late and before too much damage is done.

I'm sure there are many others out there who express their concerns and offer their expertise for the benefit of our country. I join with them in echoing my concerns and commitment for this country we love. There are other concerns I have over our country that, at another time and place or if given the opportunity, I will share with whoever will listen.

In the reading and editing of this book, I've realized that there are a number of issues that were duplicated and repeated. I considered condensing the best of what I was trying to say into one topical area of organized structure, but decided against it. I know that my mind was aware of the things that were being duplicated and repeated, but my passion over these things and my heart obviously felt that they needed to be repeated or expressed in a different way. I've allowed the inspiration and creativity given to me to take these issues where inspiration has led me and I feel that I should stay true to the inspiration I was given. I have learned in life that when I overlook the world's preferences and follow my heart or spiritual convictions, then things turn out for the best in the end. In writing this book, I have been more concerned about the substance of what I'm saying and an urgency of time than I have been with following proper literary etiquette and format.

The bottom line of why I'm doing this is because I have children, grandchildren, and will have great-grandchildren who will need and deserve an America that can support the kind of life we enjoyed as we grew up. I also love our country and believe it's worth saving. Ross Perot made an appeal to the American people while running for president that I have followed ever since and will never forget. He said **"vote your conscience."** I have been voting my conscience first and my party preference second ever since. I believe our Founding Fathers did this, and I aspire to follow their example of following my heart as a matter of conscience in spite of the status quo around me and what is popular. Well, I think I've said about all I can for now so I'll finish with saying I love America, our freedoms, the amazing people who sacrificed to establish our country and all those proud Americans who still preserve her today. May God continue to bless and protect us.

Sincerely,

Jeff Bradford

WORKS CITED

Skousen, Cleon. The Making of America: The Substance and

Meaning of the Constitution: 3rd Edition.   America:

National Center for Constitutional Studies, 2009. Print.

Reference: [1] page 55, [2] chapter 2, [3] chapter 8.

WORKS RESEARCHED

Skousen, Cleon. The Making of America: The Substance and

Meaning of the Constitution: 3rd Edition.   America:

National Center for Constitutional Studies, 2009. Print

Taxfoundation.org. Tax Foundation. Web. October 2011

CBO.gov. Congressional Budget Office. Web. October 2011

Census.gov U.S. Census Bureau. Web. October 2011

http://www.rense.com/general54/preco.htm

http://www.mipa.ca/big-secret-price-gouging-swindle-drug-companies-will-never-admit

My name is Jeff Bradford and this is my beautiful wife, Karen. We have six children and seven grandchildren to date. We enjoy spending time together with family and friends whenever we can. We enjoy being active in sports, boating, camping, attending plays and movies, learning, reading, our church and other personal endeavors. Thank you for reading our book. We wish you love, happiness and all the many blessings that God has in store for you.

WHAT AMERICA NEEDS TO SURVIVE

HELP TAKE AMERICA BACK!
If you agree with what you have read, then share
these ideas with everyone you know.

WWW.SAVE-AMERICA-2012.COM

See our web site at:

www.save-america-2012.com

Contact info:

saveamerica2012@hotmail.com

See our Face book page at:

http://www.facebook.com/home.php#!/pages/Jeff-

Bradford/133374996780819

www.ingramcontent.com/pod-product-compliance
Lightning Source LLC
Chambersburg PA
CBHW050348280326
41933CB00010BA/1382